ASAE & The Center for Association Leadership
1575 I Street, NW
Washington, DC 20005-1103
Phone: (202) 626-2723; (888) 950-2723 outside the metropolitan Washington, DC area
Fax: (202) 408-9634 E-mail: books@asaecenter.org

ASAE & The Center for Association Leadership work together to bring the most comprehensive collection of services and resources to association professionals.

John H. Graham IV, CAE, President and CEO, ASAE
Susan Sarfati, CAE, President and CEO, The Center for Association Leadership and Executive Vice President, ASAE
Michelle I. Mason, CAE, Vice President, Strategic Research, The Center for Association Leadership
Susan Robertson, Senior Vice President and Managing Director, ASAE & The Center for Association Leadership
Keith C. Skillman, CAE, Vice President of Publications and Editorial Director, ASAE & The Center for Association Leadership
Baron Williams, Director, Book Publishing, ASAE & The Center for Association Leadership

Interior design by CimarronDesign.com

This book is available at a special discount when ordered in bulk quantities. For information, contact the ASAE Member Service Center at (202) 371-0940. A complete catalog of titles is available on the ASAE & The Center for Association Leadership Web site at
www.asaecenter.org/bookstore.

Library of Congress Cataloging-in-Publication Data:

American Society of Association Executives.
  7 measures of success : what remarkable associations do that others
don't / ASAE and The Center for Association Leadership.
    p. cm.
  ISBN-13: 978-0-88034-272-8
  ISBN-10: 0-88034-272-2
  1. Organizational effectiveness. 2. Associations, institutions,
etc.—Management. 3. Executive ability. I. Center for Association
Leadership. II. Title.

  HD58.9.A456 2006
  658.4'01—dc22

                    2006022611

With thanks and appreciation to

Jim Collins, our mentor,

who graciously and generously shared his knowledge,

provided invaluable insights,

and inspired us throughout this research project.

Contents

Foreword

By Jim Collins
Best-selling author of *Good to Great* and *Built to Last*

ASSOCIATIONS ARE the hidden glue of our society and econ-omy. Like the mortar that holds the bricks of a building in place, associations go largely unnoticed, yet they do much to hold the entire structure together. As such, associations cannot settle for being only good; they must work toward greatness. But what separates exceptional associations from good ones? What does it take to turn an association from good to great, and how can excellence be sustained?

In 2002, ASAE & The Center for Association Leadership assembled a team of association leaders into an ambitious multiyear effort to address exactly these questions. "If you're serious about understanding what makes for great associations," I urged, "someone in the association world should undertake a matched-pair study."

One of my mentors, Jerry Porras, conceived of the historical matched-pair method at Stanford University in the late 1980s, when we were working as research colleagues puzzling over a vexing question. If you look over 100 years of history, most well run companies adopt most of the same basic practices, and yet few become great. It doesn't matter whether you are looking at the principles of scientific management, statistical quality control, management by objectives,

Six Sigma, decentralization, reengineering, or strategic planning; the best practices tend to spread across all major companies.

Yet some companies become truly great, while others do not. The obvious question is: Why? If most companies eventually adopt largely the same practices, then what enduring principles do in fact distinguish those that become great from those that do not?

Research that examines only successful outcomes contains a fundamental flaw, what Porras called the "discover buildings trap." If you study highly successful public corporations, you'll see that they all occupy buildings, but you would equally see that 100 percent of mediocre performers also occupy buildings. The critical question is not what successful organizations share in common but what *distinguishes* great organizations from their less-successful counterparts.

In response to this dilemma, Porras had a significant research insight: Apply the idea of "twin studies" to social systems, not just in a snapshot, but over time. (In a genetic twin study, you examine the life trajectories of twins separated at birth to glean insight into nature versus nurture.) Most industries give us at least one pair of twins—two companies born in the same era, with the same market opportunities, facing the same demographics, technology shifts, and socioeconomic trends. But when you fast-forward the tape of history, some companies become great while their twin brothers and sisters do not.

Consider General Electric (GE) and Westinghouse. Both companies came into existence near the start of the 20th century. Both had access to capital and faced a gigantic opportunity to disseminate electrical power. Yet, by the end of the 20th century, GE and Westinghouse had become very different companies. GE became an icon of excellence; Westinghouse, while a successful company, failed to attain the same stature. Porras' idea was to study rigorously selected industrial twins (matched pairs) over a long enough period of time to separate short-term variables—such as luck, a single charismatic leader, or a great idea—from timeless principles that distinguish exceptional organizations from merely good ones.

Porras' methodological insight guided our six-year research effort that led to the book *Built to Last* and inspired the method behind the five-year effort that led to *Good to Great*.

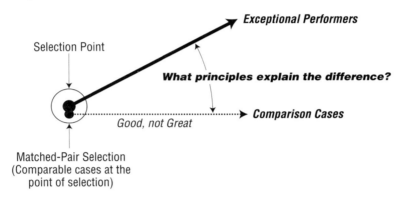

Shortly after we published *Good to Great*, I had dinner with Morten Hansen, a former member of the research team who had become a professor at Harvard. He stumped me with this question: "What is the most significant idea to come from the research so far?"

I thought about it for a minute and then offered two possibilities: Level 5 Leadership—leaders who display a paradoxical blend of personal humility and professional will—and Preserve the Core/Stimulate Progress—the discipline to hold core values and mission constant while endlessly adapting operating practices and strategies to a changing world.

"No, I don't think so," pushed Hansen. "Try again."

I mentioned a couple of other concepts from our work and he again said, "No, I don't think so."

"What do you think?" I finally asked.

"The research method itself," he said. "It could be applied to any sector of society and to almost any social question."

Inspired by Hansen's observation, we began to challenge leaders throughout the social sectors that they could—indeed, *should*—do matched-pair analyses, to answer their own questions: what systematically separates great schools, hospitals, universities, police departments, associations, orchestras, or any other set of entities from merely good ones?

But we encountered a problem. This type of research requires at least three times more effort than studying highly successful organizations by themselves. Many social sector leaders expressed interest, but most backed away when they realized that this research requires not months but *years* of effort.

Not so for ASAE & The Center for Association Leadership which, to my knowledge, became the first group to take on the challenge of applying our research method to a social sector question. During a four-year period (2002–2006), The Center's team persisted with the research project, an effort made all the more remarkable by the fact that most team members volunteered.

The team made four trips to my office in Boulder, Colorado, to discuss research progress. My own involvement in the study was limited to serving as an informal mentor, giving the research team pointers the way a faculty advisor might guide a particularly dedicated doctoral student working on a thesis. And, like a thesis advisor, the professor can take no credit for the work of the student. The team put in the thousands of hours and gave up time away from their work and families. The team selected the study set, gathered the data, sifted the evidence, and drew the conclusions. Credit for this work goes entirely to them.

The power of The Center's research lies not just in what the team found but equally in what it did *not* find. I've always enjoyed the Sherlock Holmes story *The Adventure of Silver Blaze*, wherein Holmes cracked the case with the "curious incident of the dog in the night-time." But the dog did nothing in the night-time! Ah, *that* was the curious incident—the fact that the dog did not bark—which led Holmes to the conclusion that the criminal must have been someone who knew the dog well.

In matched-pair analysis, the "dogs that do not bark" provide as much insight as positive discovery. Board size did not bark in this study. Democratic board selection did not bark. Outside professional management did not bark. The distinction between staff-driven versus member-driven did not bark; what matters is being obsessively *data*-driven, combined with the creativity and discipline to act on that data in ways that meet your members' needs better than any other organization.

Disciplined people who engage in disciplined thought and who take disciplined action—this simple mantra captures much of what separates any great institution from the average. In this report, ASAE & The Center for Association Leadership research team shines a light on the disciplines peculiar to associations. But even more important, the team issues a challenge. For implicit within the matched-pair method we find a central truth: Some organizations perform better than others, despite facing comparable opportunities and circumstances.

Every association can deliver better results for its members. The research team has done the community of associations a tremendous service by undertaking this research. Now it is up to you to make your association better tomorrow than it is today, better the next day than tomorrow, every single day, forever.

  – Jim Collins
   Boulder, Colorado
   June 10, 2006

Preface

A M I running my association in the best possible way?
You, like many other association executives, probably grapple with that question at least once a day, if not once an hour. We're always looking for the product, the strategy, the approach that makes our organizations more efficient, more effective and above all, more successful.

Over the years, countless books, magazine articles, journals, meetings, conference sessions, and other resources have contributed to the building of an impressive store of knowledge related to association management. In fact, the profession itself has outlined that body of knowledge and developed a certification exam to assess whether someone demonstrates it.

Much of what we know about association management, however, is not based on empirical data. Rather, it is based on common sense, as well as individual and collective experience. This anecdotal information has given rise to numerous, oft-repeated "conventional wisdoms" about our profession that may—or may not—stand up under scientific scrutiny.

A Useful Model

In 1994, Jim Collins gained national attention with the publication of *Built to Last*. Co-authored by Jerry Porras, the book addressed one basic question: What makes the truly exceptional companies *different* from other companies?

After identifying highly visionary companies through a jurying process, Collins and Porras matched each one to a control organization. For example, American Express, a visionary company, was matched with Wells Fargo. Then, for each pair, they carefully examined a massive amount of information about each company. In the process, they identified basic concepts or successful habits that set the visionary companies apart from others.

Ever the curious researcher, Collins reflected on the fact that the visionary companies profiled in *Built to Last* had always been great. So what factors would transform a good company into a great one? A desire to answer that compelling question prompted Collins' next book, *Good to Great*. In it, he employed a methodology similar to what he and Porras had used before, including matched research pairs. For each great company, he selected a counterpart in the same industry that had had the same opportunities and similar resources but had failed to make the long-term transition from good to great.

Several of the findings reported in *Good to Great,* such as the need to focus on the core mission, resonated with the association community. Others were more problematic. For example, Collins found that great organizations "get the right people on the bus." But most associations and nonprofit organizations have a shared management responsibility between staff and volunteers; no one individual within an association has the same latitude as a corporate CEO to get people on or off the team.

Early in 2002, several members of The Center for Association Leadership's Research Committee, (formerly the ASAE Foundation) heard Collins speak at a conference called Digital Now in Orlando,

Florida. They agreed that, while not all of the results applied to associations, the methodology used in *Good to Great* certainly had value. Even better, Collins enthusiastically supported the idea that the methodology he had used could help identify what made outstanding associations different from others.

Teaming Up

Thanks to the efforts of Hugh Lee of Fusion Productions, several committee members had the opportunity to meet with Collins at his office in Boulder, Colorado. The office is a converted school building—in fact, the conference room occupies a portion of Collins' old first-grade classroom.

In his first-grade report card, which is framed and hanging on the wall, Collins' teacher had noted, "Jimmy is a nice boy and plays well with others"—a trait that he has never lost. Greeting us with warmth and enthusiasm, Jim quickly put us at ease. Within minutes, we were knee-deep in a discussion of an association research project.

From the outset, Collins agreed to mentor us through the research process. He was interested in seeing others replicate his work in their own environments, while we were interested in finding our own answers. Thus began our partnership. Much like a professor providing guidance to doctoral students, Collins would serve as our advisor. He would ensure we remained true to his research methodology and provide a structure for us to follow along with advice when needed. The actual work, however—from start to finish—would be our own.

Willingness to Share

The Measures of Success Project, as it came to be known, was the first internal research project undertaken completely by The Center for Association Leadership. It involved many years of staff time, countless hours of volunteer time, and several moments of spirited discussion and debate.

This research project would not have come to fruition, however, without the participation of the associations profiled in the pages of this book. Those that served as our research "study group" are clearly identified. As truly exceptional organizations, they rose above the rest in many ways.

Keep in mind, however, that the associations paired with the study group for comparison purposes are also strong performers. They simply did not rise to the same level of greatness during the 15 years prior to and including 2003 that we chose as the focus of this study. We were looking for the qualities or factors that explained the differences between the two groups—or, as Collins would say, what made one association a gold-medal winner and what made its comparison organization a silver- or bronze-medal winner.

In some cases, as with Olympic performances when only a second or two may separate the winners of the gold and silver medals, the difference was not that great. In fact, had the time period being studied been slightly different, several associations in the comparison group may well have been contenders for the study group. To keep attention focused on the aggregate results, we decided not to publicly identify the organizations that served as the comparison half of the matched pairs.

Agreeing to participate in the study was no small commitment for organizations in either research group. While Collins relied on public documents for much of his work, we had to ask the participating organizations to gather and supply membership and financial data, not to mention information about leadership, staffing, operations, governance, culture, products, and markets. Researchers and task force members also conducted on-site interviews that required a considerable time commitment from the organizations visited.

Because associations in both the study and comparison groups opened their doors and their books to the task force, we had the opportunity to see what the differences are. Some differences are subtle; others are dramatic. All offer considerable food for thought.

At one point during the research process, when the end was not yet in sight, Collins provided this reassurance: "Do your work right, and it will be timeless." If we have achieved that goal, it is because he was our mentor, our guide, and, at times, our cheerleader.

Through his work, Collins clearly demonstrated that, through careful study and analysis, one could discover what made great companies different from good ones. We hope we have done the same for associations and, in the process, contributed to the advancement of our profession.

Michael E. Gallery, Ph.D., CAE
President, OPIS, LLC, and Chair, Measures of Success
Task Force (2002–2006)

Susan Sarfati, CAE
President and Chief Executive Officer, The Center for
Association Leadership, and Executive Vice President,
American Society of Association Executives

Contributors

A s members of The Center for Association Leadership's Measures of Success Task Force, the following individuals contributed countless hours to reviewing data, preparing analyses and reports, and engaging in wide-ranging discussions. This book represents the culmination of their efforts during the course of several years.

James G. Dalton, president, Strategic Counsel, Derwood, Maryland

Phyllis L. Edans, CPA, CAE, chief financial officer, American College of Emergency Physicians, Irving, Texas

Michael E. Gallery, Ph.D., CAE, president and founder, OPIS, LLC, Highland Village, Texas (chair of the task force)

Mark J. Golden, CAE, executive director and chief executive officer, National Court Reporters Association, Vienna, Virginia

Richard B. Green, vice president of association sales, Marriott International, Inc., Washington, D.C.

Wayne H. Gross, CAE, Smyrna, Georgia

Pamela Hemann, CAE, president, Association Management Services, Inc., Pasadena, California

Wells B. Jones, CFRE, CAE, chief executive officer, Guide Dog Foundation for the Blind, Smithtown, New York

Sherry L. Keramidas, Ph.D., CAE, executive director, Regulatory Affairs Professionals Society, Rockville, Maryland

Hugh K. Lee, president, Fusion Productions, Webster, New York

Dawn M. Mancuso, CAE, MAM, executive director and chief executive officer, Association of Air Medical Services, Alexandria, Virginia

Michelle I. Mason, CAE, vice president of strategic research, The Center for Association Leadership, Washington, D.C.

David J. Noonan, deputy executive vice president, American Academy of Ophthalmology, San Francisco, California

Sandra R. Sabo, writer and editor, Sandra R. Sabo Editorial Services, Mendota Heights, Minnesota

Sarah J. Sanford, CAE, executive director, Society of Actuaries, Schaumburg, Illinois

Susan Sarfati, CAE, president and chief executive officer, The Center for Association Leadership, and executive vice president, ASAE, Washington, D.C.

Acknowledgments

THIS BOOK represents the fruit of almost four years' labor. From September 2002 through January 2006, under the diligent chairmanship of Michael E. Gallery, Ph.D., CAE, members of the Measures of Success Task Force reviewed mountains of documents, analyzed spreadsheets, and engaged in numerous discussions about what the data were really saying. Dr. Gallery's tireless leadership and vision were instrumental in bringing this project to completion.

This effort offered the best learning opportunity of task force members' professional careers. All appreciate ASAE & The Center for Association Leadership's support of this important contribution to the association community.

The task force's work would not have been possible without the staff of ASAE & The Center for Association Leadership, notably Michelle Mason. As vice president of research programs, she shepherded the Measures of Success project through all its stages, from concept to execution, and ensured it remained on track no matter what obstacles arose. She also served as the liaison to Jim Collins and his organization.

Collins encouraged the task force and staff to bring "the curiosity of chimps" to the project, which included several "chimposiums," meetings focused on exploring the intriguing questions raised by the research. The groundwork for these meetings was laid by Elizabeth Farner and Bradley Feuling. Hired by ASAE & The Center as much for their curiosity as for their educational credentials, Farner and Feuling doggedly tracked down information by phone, via the Internet, and in person; conducted interviews with a wide range of association personnel, from CEOs to receptionists; and produced pages upon pages of spreadsheet analyses. When both Farner and Fueling headed to graduate school, their successor, Anna Cruz, matched their talents and perseverance.

Before beginning on-site visits to the participating organizations, Farner and Fueling finalized the questions and honed their interviewing skills at four task force members' organizations. Most deserving of thanks for serving as "beta test sites"—although not included in the study—are the American Academy of Ophthalmology, American College of Emergency Physicians, Guide Dog Foundation for the Blind, and Regulatory Affairs Professionals Society.

To help task force members review and process the data amassed by staff, Sara Wedeman, Ph.D., founder of Behavioral Economics Consulting Group, LLC, developed online tools to aid the interviewing process and provided statistical analysis. Wedeman's familiarity with Collins' concepts as well as her ability to succinctly summarize trends within the data contributed to the success of the task force's final chimposium.

A special thank you goes to Sandy Sabo, freelance writer and editor, who converted a mixture of task force members' thoughts, observations, discussions, and conclusions into a cohesive manuscript.

A final note of appreciation goes to all donors of The Center for Association Leadership (See Appendix G). Thanks to their generous financial support, The Center was able to undertake this comprehensive, ground-breaking research project that will have ramifications for many years to come.

CHAPTER I

A Study of Differences

EMPTING THOUGH it may be, you can't write an equation for success in an association. Too many factors come into play: developments in the industry or profession, the economy, the leadership style of staff and volunteers, and the needs of the members themselves, to name just a few. Even if one association achieves success by doing A, B, and C, there's no guarantee that another association, following the same equation, will enjoy the same result.

That said, some factors undoubtedly show up more frequently than others among successful associations. These organizations are highly efficient as well as highly effective. They not only provide products and services of value to their members but also do so at the right time, in the right way, and at the right cost. In short, they know what needs to be done, and they do it well.

But what factors truly set successful associations apart from others? What unique characteristics do they, as a group, share that makes them *different* from other associations? Those are the questions at the heart of the long-term research project undertaken by The Center for Association Leadership, which culminates in this book. For nearly four years, staff and volunteers gathered and reviewed data, conducted interviews and site visits, and tested hypotheses. They eventually identified seven factors that were common to the most successful associations that participated in the study.

◆ ◆ ◆ ◆ ◆ ◆ ◆

THE 7 MEASURES OF SUCCESS

Commitment to Purpose
1. A Customer Service Culture
2. Alignment of Products and Services with Mission

Commitment to Analysis and Feedback
3. Data-Driven Strategies
4. Dialogue and Engagement
5. CEO as a Broker of Ideas

Commitment to Action
6. Organizational Adaptability
7. Alliance Building

Here's the path the research committee took to arrive at *7 Measures of Success: What Remarkable Associations Do That Others Don't.*

The First Steps

The Measures of Success Task Force began its work in early 2003. First on the agenda was generating the list of great associations from which both the study and comparison groups would be drawn. In *Good to Great*, Collins had used stock price to determine which companies made the cut for his study. This objective measure has no equivalent in the association sector. Therefore, the task force followed the jurying process that Collins and Porras had employed when researching *Built to Last*.

The American Society of Association Executives (ASAE) generated a random, nth-name sample of 1,000 CEOs, number-two executives, and industry leaders within its membership database. These executives received an explanatory letter and a request to nominate, in rank order, their choices for the top five associations in the country. Two follow-up mailings and a reminder postcard contributed to a response rate of 32 percent; this represents a 95 percent confidence level for sampling error.

The list generated by the survey respondents numbered 506 associations. The top 104 associations—those mentioned most frequently by respondents—received invitations to participate in the Measures of Success project, along with a request for preliminary data related to finances, membership, leadership, and organizing structure. Of the 51 associations that responded to this initial mailing (a 49 percent response rate), 82 percent indicated their interest in participating. Any association with a close connection to the project, such as a staff member serving on the task force, was disqualified from consideration.

While the survey was in progress, The Center for Association Leadership hired two full-time research investigators, both recent college graduates. Collins had suggested taking this approach to getting much of the work done because he has employed it himself. In Collins' view, recent graduates are accustomed to working hard and typically bring an active curiosity to digging through data to unearth nuggets of valuable information. In fact, he praised his research investigators for being "chimps"—a reference to Curious George, the fictitious character in children's storybooks, whose insatiable urge to discover more about the world led to many adventures.

Also with guidance from Collins, task force members developed criteria to apply to the potential participants and identified the period of study as the 15 years preceding and including 2003. The criteria were selected to reduce the likelihood that any findings of the study could be attributed to a particular characteristic or circumstance, such as a CEO with tenure over the entire span of the study, or an anomaly, such as an economic downturn within the association's trade or profession.

To be eligible for consideration for either the study or comparison groups an association needed to have:

- Been in operation for at least 20 years;
- Finished more years in the black than in the red;
- Exhibited the ability to retain members, donors, or market share during the study period;
- Had more than one CEO during the study period.

In addition to meeting these criteria, an association had to be willing to fully cooperate in the research process. That meant providing detailed, often confidential, financial and membership information; submitting reams of paper, including publications, annual reports, and meeting minutes; hosting site visits; and answering numerous questions about its policies, procedures, and internal operations.

This cooperation on the part of the research subjects marks one area of departure from Collins' work. Where he had access to public documents detailing financial performance, for example, the task force relied on the associations' cooperation to provide the data. Collins conducted his research with the full awareness, if not the cooperation, of the companies being studied; the Measures of Success Task Force needed associations to provide both.

Another limitation to participation was an association's ability to provide the appropriate data. Several associations, despite their desire to participate, had to withdraw from the study because they either did not have the staff resources necessary to generate all the data requested or did not have complete data for the full study period. Other groups were excused from the study because the task force was unable to find suitable associations to form a matched pair.

Making the Lists

Once the research investigators had gathered preliminary data for review, the task force began the process of selecting which organizations to study in depth. The intent was to include all types of organizations (trade, professional, philanthropic), reflect various geographic scopes (state, national, international), and represent various membership sizes (small, medium, large).

Several associations immediately stood out as having performed consistently in the black and having maintained a consistent member/donor base during the study period; in addition, all had received frequent mentions by the ASAE members who participated in the jurying process. These became candidates for the study group of remarkable associations.

Ultimately, the study group was composed of these nine organizations (See Appendix A for organizational profiles):

- AARP
- American College of Cardiology
- American Dental Association
- Associated General Contractors of America
- Girl Scouts of the USA
- National Association of Counties
- Ohio Society of Certified Public Accountants
- Radiological Society of North America
- Society for Human Resource Management

To identify suitable candidates for the comparison group, the task force looked for associations that were similar to the study group in terms of budget and staff size, type (such as individual membership organization), and geographic scope. Whenever possible, efforts were made to match organizations that had similar missions or served similar memberships.

For the most part, the task force selected the nine members of the comparison group from the list of 105 organizations generated by the jurying process. In two instances, the task force cast its net wider to locate a better match for a study group.

The major differences between the study and comparison groups rested with their respective performances on the selection criteria, primarily those related to financial health and membership retention. In other words, associations in the comparison group were similar in all major respects to their counterparts in the study group, except that they had experienced fewer years in the black and/or had higher membership attrition rates.

All the associations studied—no matter which group they were placed in—were strong performers. The aim of the Measures of Success project was to compare remarkable and good associations, not good and bad ones. The project's value lies in discerning the often subtle differences between two well-matched organizations—what one association did or didn't do to give it a performance or financial edge on its counterpart.

Data Gathering and Analysis

Having placed 18 organizations into matched pairs, the task force outlined the areas for comparison and analysis. Once again drawing on the methodology employed by Collins and Porras in *Built to Last*, the task force selected 11 variables to identify differences among groups:

1. Vision (core values, mission, purpose, goals)
2. Markets, Competitors, and the Environment
3. Organizational Arrangements (structure, policies, systems)
4. Use of Technology
5. Business Strategy
6. Products and Services
7. Leadership (staff, elected)

8. Community and Culture
9. Financial Health
10. Physical Setting and Location
11. Public Policy

The Center for Association Leadership partnered with a specialist in behavioral research who guided the development of both a process and a set of tools that included multiple data inputs, in multiple formats. We structured the process and the instruments together. This ensured they were consistent in focus and could be related to one another, with the variables serving as a least common denominator, even though the nature of the information differed (structured, quantitative versus open-ended, qualitative).

In both design and implementation, we adhered to a high professional standard for conducting behavioral research that involves collecting data of multiple types, through multiple media, then testing them against the hypotheses developed at the outset. In other words, we were testing to see which variables were most closely associated with sustained, outstanding organizational performance.

The task force employed the following process:

Develop goals and overall plan with Jim Collins.

Conduct review of published literature.

Develop list of variables and project plan.

Develop standard topic guide and information request for all participants.

Develop 12 structured, web-based data collection instruments for recording quantitative and qualitative feedback.

Review, organize, synthesize, analyze information; conduct 'reality checks.'

The two research investigators conducted a field test of the interview questions at four associations that had representation on the task force. Feedback from these test experiences led to revisions in the structured interview process.

Armed with data-gathering instruments, including checklists and lists of questions, the research investigators conducted on-site interviews at the nine organizations in the study group and the nine organizations in the comparison group. In all cases, they spoke with the CEO; other interviewees typically included senior and support staff representing a range of tenure at the association. These interviews were transcribed and attached to the detailed report prepared for each of the 18 associations.

In addition, each participating organization submitted, on average, three large boxes of documents—financial statements, 990 forms, annual reports, examples of products, publications, marketing plans, results of membership surveys, minutes of board meetings, and so forth. The research investigators used the financial data to generate charts and graphs that provided a historical perspective of net revenue, net profitability, ratio of net assets to total expenses, membership attrition, and level of reserves.

Once this data-gathering process concluded, the material needed to be reviewed through the eyes of association professionals. At this point, two task force members were assigned to each matched pair and given the task of studying the financial data, written reports, interview transcripts, and all the materials submitted by the associations. They became, in essence, experts on their two assigned groups. Each team made at least one visit to ASAE & The Center for Association Leadership's headquarters, where the submitted materials were kept to maintain confidentiality. (All members of the task force and others involved in the research process signed confidentiality agreements.)

To guide the evaluation teams through the massive amounts of information collected, Collins offered a framework for analysis. He posed three questions that became the basis of each team's approach to formulating conclusions about the data:

- What did you find that ran counter to conventional wisdom?
- What did all the organizations share in common? In other words, what are the necessities for any organization to be considered good?
- What major factors accounted for the differences between the study and comparison groups?

After compiling an extensive list of conventional wisdoms related to association management (See Appendix D) and discussing the other two questions, the task force realized some necessary information was still missing. One representative from each team agreed to conduct a follow-up, on-site visit, including an interview with each CEO, to fill in the gaps and to get a better feel for each organization's culture and physical setting. A structured set of interview questions was developed to ensure that each team member asked the same questions, in the same order (See Appendix C).

After completing the supplemental data collection, each team member wrote an individual dossier that analyzed the similarities and differences between the two groups. Next, the two members of each team pooled their thoughts and prepared one team dossier for distribution to the other task force members (See Appendix C).

In January 2006, the task force convened to review all nine dossiers. This book presents the results of the discussions and debates that the task force engaged in to identify commonalities and differences across the groups and to put conventional wisdoms to the test.

Probability Versus Proof

Contrary to popular opinion, science does not deal with proof. Rather, it deals with prediction. The purpose of scientific research is to explain relationships and then predict the outcome of future events based on observation of the data.

Rarely can you say with certainty that one particular event or action causes a particular outcome. Usually, an outcome is caused by a combination of several variables acting together. Understanding the relationship among the variables enables you to predict outcomes.

For example, some critics have noted that research has never proven that smoking causes cancer. It takes only one exception to the hypothesis to disprove it: one smoker who never develops cancer. But researchers have demonstrated that people who smoke are more likely to develop cancer than those who do not smoke.

Moreover, people with a family history of cancer have a greater likelihood of developing the disease, compared to those without that history. When these two factors—family history and smoking—are combined, the chances of developing cancer increase even more. You can predict, with a higher level of confidence, the likelihood of cancer.

The Measures of Success Task Force wanted to identify the factors remarkable organizations shared in common, as distinct from the comparison group. To what degree any of these caused an association to be remarkable was outside the scope of the study. But by identifying the measures related to remarkable organizations, we could develop a means for predicting the likelihood that other organizations which possess the same attributes may also become remarkable.

To identify predictors of remarkable associations, we used a 2×2 analysis table. Suppose, for example, you wanted to determine if eye color is related to hair color. If you have 10 people with blond hair and 10 with brown hair, the 2×2 analysis table might look like this:

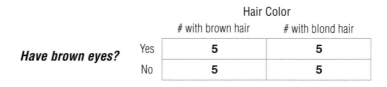

		Hair Color	
		# with brown hair	# with blond hair
Have brown eyes?	Yes	5	5
	No	5	5

By pure chance alone, you'd expect that each cell would contain five individuals. In that case, you'd conclude that there is no relationship between the color of hair and the color of eyes. If, however, the majority of brown-haired people have brown eyes and the majority of blond-haired people do not, you'd conclude that there *is* a relationship between hair color and eye color.

We used the same logic to determine which factors, if any, were related to remarkable associations. For each measure—for example, a customer service culture—we asked if it were observed in both the study and the comparison groups. Based on pure chance, you'd expect that half of the organizations in both groups would exhibit a certain factor and half would not. In such a case, there would be no relationship between a certain measure and remarkable associations. If, however, the distribution was greater than expected by chance, it would point to a relationship.

Measures observed in at least six or more of the study group and *not* observed in fewer than six in the comparison group were determined to be characteristics of the remarkable group but not characteristics of the comparison group. To meet our criterion, the 2×2 table for any measure had to appear, at a minimum, like the sample below.

Measure: Customer Service Culture

		# of Study Organizations	# of Comparison Organizations
Demonstrated a customer service culture?	Yes	6	4
	No	4	6

This logic formed the basis for the identification of research results. Any factor displayed by a majority of the study group, but not displayed by a majority of the comparison group, was selected. It is also important to note that several variables may exist beyond those we identified. Nevertheless, these seven measures of success are unique among the study group and, therefore, are associated with remarkable associations.

In all cases, the team dossiers confirmed that all 18 organizations had been placed in the appropriate group, whether study or comparison. For all nine pairings, the associations in the study group outperformed their counterparts in the comparison group in a majority of areas. That's not to say there weren't bright spots among the comparison group; in fact, in several instances, those associations performed almost as well as their counterparts in the study group.

The task force's discussions uncovered both positive and negative correlations within and among the study and comparison groups. Again and again, the task force revisited these correlations, some of which withstood repeated scrutiny. Others did not, either because they were not present in a majority of the pairings or because the evidence was not overwhelming enough to substantiate them. Likewise, some conventional wisdom held true for the groups studied; other commonly held beliefs appeared to have shaky foundations.

More clarity emerged each time task force members asked, "What factors are most likely to lead to an association being remarkable?" In the end, they made judgment calls based on financial data, interviews, site visits, reviews of materials, and their own experiences as association executives.

The Commitments

Eventually, three years of data gathering and analysis culminated in the identification of seven factors, or measures of success, that differentiate remarkable associations from their counterparts. These characteristics are deeply ingrained in the study group's organizational DNA. They represent commitments consistently honored by the organization, not just intentions, aspirations, or marketing messages.

Commitment to Purpose

A Customer Service Culture

Alignment of Products and Services with Mission

Remarkable

Data-Driven Strategies

Organizational Adaptability

Alliance Building

Dialogue and Engagement

CEO as a Broker of Ideas

Commitment to Action

Commitment to Analysis and Feedback

In the chapters that follow, you'll find detailed explanations and examples of the seven measures. No one measure outweighs the others; all contribute equally to an association's ability to innovate, grow, and thrive over time. They are not presented in any particular order or priority but rather are grouped into three categories.

Each association in the study group exemplified these seven measures of success:

Commitment to Purpose

A Customer Service Culture—A "we're here to serve you" approach not only permeates all individual encounters with members but also is built into organizational structure and processes.

Alignment of Products and Services with Mission—The depth and breadth of offerings are consistent with the organization's mission, which remains central and unchanging even in the midst of changes in the external environment.

Commitment to Analysis and Feedback

Data-Driven Strategies—Remarkable associations have developed an expertise in gathering information as well as processes for sharing and analyzing the data to deduce what actions the data point to taking.

Dialogue and Engagement—An internal conversation continually occurs among staff and volunteers about the organization's direction and priorities.

CEO as a Broker of Ideas—Although the CEO may be visionary, what's more important is that the CEO facilitates visionary thinking throughout the organization.

Commitment to Action

Organizational Adaptability—Remarkable associations learn from and respond to change; although willing to change, they also know what *not* to change.

Alliance Building—Associations that are secure and confident in their own right seek partners and projects that complement their mission and purpose.

Just a Sample

Please keep in mind that the nine associations in the study group simply represent a sample of exemplary associations. They are not the only nine associations that know how to achieve stellar success, nor are they the only ones that deserve to be labeled as "great" or "remarkable." No doubt other associations have registered equal or greater success in their ability to serve members and maintain a healthy financial status.

As a group, the nine study associations provide a glimpse into the world of greatness and offer seven points of entry. These seven measures of success are not intended to provide an equation for every association to follow to the letter. In fact, although all associations within the study group exhibit the seven factors, each one does so in a unique way. For example, the Radiological Society of North America and the Girl Scouts of the USA look and operate differently on the surface. But internally, both organizations have made the same commitments to purpose, analysis and feedback, and action.

The seven factors *are* intended to provide guidance, and perhaps inspiration, for both staff and volunteers who have a desire to improve their association's performance and register even greater success.

CHAPTER 2

Setting the Stage

ONDUCTING RIGOROUS, objective research about what makes remarkable associations is challenging, a fact which may contribute to the scarcity of such research in the association world.

Much of what we know about association management is based on anecdotal evidence, personal experience, common sense, and research from business and other sectors. There are obvious limitations in relying solely on these sources of information. First, the information gleaned from these sources often applies to particular situations. Generalizing from one situation to another can be problematic; an approach that works for one association may be a failure for another group. You risk investing your association's scarce resources—including time, money, attention, and effort—in popular solutions that sound good but make no difference in the long run.

Objective research is one of the most effective ways to learn which behaviors, actions, and attitudes have strategic impact on an organization and its success. That was the rationale for the general approach and methodology used by the Measures of Success Task Force of The Center for Association Leadership as it attempted to discover what constitutes success in a voluntary association.

Intellectual Foundations

From the beginning, the task force carefully reviewed and embraced the rigorous research underpinning the books *Built to Last* and *Good to Great*. Jim Collins and Jerry Porras understood the essential yet intangible relationship among core beliefs and practices and an organization's soul. As mission-driven organizations, associations depend on such beliefs and practices.

What makes the truly exceptional companies similar to one another, and what differentiates them from other companies? This question became the basis of *Built to Last*. Collins and Porras set out to learn about the visionary company, one that succeeds across generations, changes in leadership, and product lifecycles. *Built to Last*, the product of this research, focuses on industrial titans such as Boeing, IBM, Sony, Procter & Gamble, and Merck, all founded before 1950.

Of the 36 companies Collins and Porras studied, 18 were considered visionaries, while another 18 formed a comparison group. They compared each of the 18 truly exceptional companies—as measured by longevity, consistently strong performance, and superior financial results—with a prominent and successful, but less remarkable, competitor.

Collins and Porras found that organizations with vision have a much higher likelihood of enduring success. Defining vision as a global statement of *who we are* and *where we are headed,* the authors identified four key elements of vision: core ideology; core purpose; big, hairy, audacious goals (highly ambitious goals that reflect the vision); and a vivid description of the goal. In *Built to Last*, the authors also challenge much conventional wisdom propounded by venerable schools of business, pundits, and the like.

In his next book, *Good to Great*, Collins focused on companies that had started out good and had transformed themselves into great companies. What, he wondered, had they done to distinguish themselves from those that remained good?

For the research that led to *Good to Great*, Collins required an objective measure. Accordingly, the research team analyzed the stock performance of Fortune 500 companies. Among these, they identified 11 companies that had first achieved and then maintained dramatic increases in their stock price(s) while other companies in their industries had maintained good, but not spectacular, increases in stock price.

For each great company, Collins selected a counterpart company in the same industry, one that had experienced the same opportunities and similar resources but had not transformed itself from good to great. These counterpart companies formed the comparison group.

Together, *Built to Last* and *Good to Great* identified a framework of concepts that correlate with great companies in contrast to merely good ones. Those concepts are:

Level 5 Leadership. Level 5 leaders are ambitious first and foremost for the cause, the organization, the work—not themselves—and they have the fierce resolve to do whatever it takes to fulfill that ambition. A Level 5 leader displays a paradoxical blend of personal humility and professional will.

First Who, Then What. Those who build great organizations make sure they have the right people on the bus, the wrong people off the bus, and the right people in the key seats before they figure out where to drive the bus. They always think first about who and then about what.

Confront the Brutal Facts (The Stockdale Paradox). Retain unwavering faith that you can and will prevail in the end, regardless of the difficulties, and at the same time have the discipline to confront the most brutal facts of the current reality.

Hedgehog Concept. Greatness comes about by a series of good decisions consistent with a simple, coherent concept. This hedgehog is an operating model that reflects understanding of three intersecting circles: what you can be the best in world at, what you are deeply passionate about, and what best drives your economic or resource engine.

Culture of Discipline. Disciplined people who engage in disciplined thought and take disciplined action, operating with freedom within a framework of responsibilities, are the cornerstone of a culture that creates greatness. In a culture of discipline, people do not have jobs; they have responsibilities.

The Flywheel. In building greatness, there is no single defining action, no grand program, no one killer innovation, no solitary lucky break, no miracle moment. Rather, the process resembles relentlessly pushing a giant, heavy flywheel in one direction, turn upon turn, building momentum until a point of breakthrough, and beyond.

Clock Building, Not Time Telling. Truly great organizations prosper through multiple generations of leaders—the exact opposite of being built around a single great leader, great idea, or specific program. Leaders in great organizations build catalytic mechanisms to stimulate progress and do not depend on having a charismatic personality to get things done; indeed, many had a "charisma bypass."

Preserve the Core/Stimulate Progress. Enduring great organizations are characterized by a fundamental duality. On the one hand, they have a set of timeless core values and a core reason for being that remain constant over long periods of time. On the other hand, they have a relentless drive for change and progress, a creative compulsion that often manifests in BHAGs (Big Hairy Audacious Goals). Great organizations keep clear the difference between their core values, which never change, and operating strategies and cultural practices, which endlessly adapt to a changing world.

In the work of Collins, the Measures of Success Task Force found not only a methodology that made sense from a research standpoint but also well-defined concepts that begged to be tested in the association environment.

CHAPTER 3

Commitment to Purpose

*Commitment to Purpose:
Consistently exhibiting a customer service
culture and an alignment of products and
services with organizational mission.*

How DO you measure success?

When asked that question, the CEO of one association in the study group responded, "We measure success by how relevant we are to members: Are we meeting their needs? Are we anticipating their needs?"

That member-oriented mindset and focus clearly emerged from the study group. In how they are organized and operate, the study associations always focus first on what they can do for members, by anticipating and meeting member needs.

THE 7 MEASURES OF SUCCESS

Commitment to Purpose
1. A Customer Service Culture
2. Alignment of Products and Services with Mission

Commitment to Analysis and Feedback
3. Data-Driven Strategies
4. Dialogue and Engagement
5. CEO as a Broker of Ideas

Commitment to Action
6. Organizational Adaptability
7. Alliance Building

An Association of the Members, by the Members, for the Members

Measure 1: A Customer Service Culture

Ask employees of any association why the association exists and most are likely to say, "We're here to serve our members." It's a predictable, safe response—and, in the case of remarkable associations, it also happens to be true.

Remarkable associations do not pay lip service to the idea of serving their members. On the contrary, they demonstrate their commitment to members in everything they do, from answering the phone, to responding to e-mail, to developing quality products and services. "This would be a great place to work if it weren't for the members" is the type of humorous comment often voiced by association staff. Such statements, even in jest, are never even whispered in remarkable associations.

This first measure, having **a customer service culture**, goes well beyond individual encounters with members. Remarkable associations build their structures, processes, and interactions—their

A SERVICE ORIENTATION EVIDENT EVERYWHERE

To underscore its central belief that providing excellent service to members is the responsibility of every employee, the American Dental Association (ADA) provides customer service training to all staff. In support of its overall purpose, the association also has articulated a mission and five values specifically for its employees. Here's how they read:

Mission
ADA staff are dedicated partners contributing their knowledge, experience, and expertise to support the dental profession and the people it serves.

Values
1. Members are the purpose of our work. The same is true of communities of interest and coworkers seeking assistance from us in serving our membership. We are all part of the same team, working for the same goals.
   - Membership is everybody's business.
   - Diversity adds value to our community and work.
   - Support the improvement of oral health worldwide.
   - Take pride in dentistry.

2. We take personal responsibility to ensure that all members, potential members, coworkers, and others we serve receive a timely, accurate, and courteous response to their needs.
   - Listen with intent to understand rather than merely intent to reply.
   - Freely share our knowledge.
   - Meet and exceed expectations.
   - Communicate clearly.

3. We take pride in our work.
   - Do the little things and the big things well.
   - Demonstrate zeal for finding solutions.
   - Work diligently, creatively, and effectively.
   - Demonstrate personal dignity, integrity, and dedication.

4. Attitudes are contagious.
   - Extend courtesy and compassion.
   - Be committed and professional.
   - Give praise, recognition, and appreciation often.
   - Lead by example.
   - Have fun: Enjoy our professional life.

5. We thrive in a supportive organization that...
   - Is based upon trust and mutual respect.
   - Facilitates opportunities to learn and grow.
   - Provides the necessary tools and information to do our job.
   - Treats people fairly.
   - Helps us feel that we make a difference and rewards contributions.
   - Applauds innovation and reasonable risk-taking.

entire culture—around assessing and fulfilling members' needs and expectations.

This unity of focus permeates the entire organization. Everyone—staff, leaders, and members alike—knows who the association serves and keeps the member not only at center stage but also in the spotlight. No one presumes to decide what the member needs without asking first and then listening to the answer.

Because the needs and challenges faced by members always take precedence, the way the association replies may seem contrary to its best interest. For example, Associated General Contractors (AGC) changed its dues structure when feedback from chapters indicated the structure was too complicated and the maximum dues cap was too expensive. Lowering dues meant decreasing the association's budget and, consequently, changing how it served members, but AGC took that step in recognition of its members' expressed concerns and as a means of refocusing on its mission.

Always on the Lookout

Providing excellent service to members does not translate into "We'll do everything or anything the members ask." It does mean the association makes every effort to understand the members' needs and attempts, within the confines of the mission, to meet them. It means always being on the lookout for the possibilities and opportunities presented by the members' needs and expectations.

In that regard, Girl Scouts of the USA (GSUSA) offers an interesting example. The organization never forgets whom it exists to serve—the girls. In fact, cubicles throughout its headquarters building are decorated with Girl Scouting materials, including photographs of members, as a constant reminder of its vision to "bring Girl Scouting to every girl."

Yet, while maintaining absolute clarity about its purpose, GSUSA also understands that its target population is different from its customers—the local councils that facilitate delivery of the Girl Scout program. That's why GSUSA devotes considerable resources to creating software and research monographs, among other tools, that enable the councils to operate effectively.

GSUSA continually asks, "How do we need to change in order to stay true to our mission?" So everything is subject to change, *except for the underlying values.*

Consequently, "bringing Girl Scouting to every girl" now means more than organizing traditional troops. The organization has developed flexible pathways for girls to participate, such as delivering the Girl Scout program through suburban after-school programs and urban neighborhood youth centers. Another program, "Girl Scouting in Detention Centers" offers incarcerated girls the opportunity to participate in many GSUSA activities, and "Girl Scouts Beyond Bars" facilitates visits between incarcerated mothers and daughters.

Although few people probably associate the Girl Scout purpose— "to inspire girls with the highest ideals of character"—with girls in detention centers, such programs underscore the organization's ultimate goal to always focus on the member rather than on a particular image it wants to convey.

This clarity about purpose is marked with a real pragmatism about the means necessary to achieve those ends. GSUSA is every bit as serious and tenacious about putting together the resources, talent, and expertise needed to be effective in addressing its mission as it is passionate about the mission itself. As a case in point, GSUSA's public policy and advocacy agenda explicitly addresses two categories of issues: those that directly affect girls and those that affect the organization's corporate rights.

GOING THE EXTRA MILE FOR MEMBERS

An analysis of membership acquisition and retention numbers shows that the Ohio Society of Certified Public Accountants (OSCPA) did not suffer wide swings in membership or in participation, even during periods of professional or economic upheaval, when it chose to give away more services to members. OSCPA even gives away a full year of benefits, in the form of a complimentary membership, to any individual who passes the state CPA exam.

To remind members that the association is designed to meet their professional needs, OSCPA goes to extraordinary lengths with its retention efforts. The six-step plan starts with two written notices to members who fail to renew. If necessary, these are followed by up to three personal phone calls, usually from the staff membership vice president, the CEO, and a colleague of the lapsed member. Such a level of personal contact is no small undertaking in a 23,000-member society.

As a last effort, OSCPA sends a surprise message in the form of its monthly magazine. On the outside, the magazine looks identical to the one sent to members in good standing. On the inside, however, the pages are blank except for a message directed exclusively to the lapsed member: "If you had renewed your membership, this magazine would have been full of information and articles that would interest you."

Driven by Mission, Not Money

Measure 2:
Alignment of Products and Services with Mission

The second measure of success is alignment of products and services with mission. Remarkable associations speak passionately about fulfilling their mission and constantly test their ideas for products against that mission, using it as a touchstone for everything they do.

Having a passion for the purpose, however, does not necessarily translate into proficiency. Among the comparison group, we found several instances of organizations whose employees and members exhibited powerful emotion when discussing the association's founding and raison d'être. Even though these organizations had a strong sense of who they originally were, they hadn't effectively harnessed the passion to keep driving forward. In many ways, these associations failed to link the mission to the development of strategic direction, operations, products, and services that would define who they are.

Associations in the study group consistently found ways to connect their reason for being to their programs and services. Most offered, more or less, the usual array of meetings, trade shows, professional publications, educational programs, and affinity programs. Yet while the depth, breadth, and nature of the products and services varied from one remarkable association to another, what didn't change was the consistent focus on linking those offerings to their mission. That focus rarely wavered, even as external forces, societal changes, and developments within the membership itself occurred. In this regard, great associations are truly member-driven.

At GSUSA, for example, the staff and leaders always ask the same central question: What do girls need *today* for us to achieve the mission we have always had? New initiatives and changes to existing programs and services flow from there.

Consider the Radiological Society of North America (RSNA). At one time, RSNA provided association management services to 21 related subgroups or specialties. A few years ago, RSNA determined that being in the association management business was a diversion from its mission to educate radiologists and to support radiological research. It took the disciplined but controversial action of releasing all but the three academic societies that were deemed central to its core purpose. The three societies, which focus on advancing radiology in careers, research, and education, now form an academic council within RSNA.

An organization in the comparison group found itself in a similar situation of managing special interest groups within the membership. With the association unwilling or unable to decide what to do about these groups, they continue to drain its economic reserves, organizational energy, and staff attention. Hence, the association has lost the focus on its mission that is needed to achieve greatness.

A Good Fit

Aligning their offerings with their mission enables great associations to do the right things well, even if they fall short on their outcome measures. Make no mistake: Remarkable associations hit their numbers. But they consider themselves successful only if they serve member needs and make progress toward their vision while hitting the numbers.

Remarkable associations view members as a population to serve rather than a market to sell to. In fact, they reject out-of-hand a product or service that fails to directly aid their members, even if it might generate revenue.

The National Association of Counties (NACo) is one organization that is completely driven by its commitment to meet member needs. If it makes money, so much the better. As one employee noted, "The purpose of a program is the greater good: How can we help counties? Nobody is going to rule out anything that at least meets that criteria."

One of NACo's success stories is the U.S. Communities Government Purchasing Alliance (GPA), which it cosponsors with the Association of School Business Officials International, National Institute of Governmental Purchasing, National League of Cities, and United States Conference of Mayors. GPA grew out of the recognition that counties are chronically short of money. It enables local government agencies to aggregate their purchasing power and obtain volume pricing on office supplies, technology products, janitorial supplies, park equipment, and other categories of supplies. NACo probably could have crafted a group purchasing arrangement on a much smaller scale, such as a typical affinity services program. Doing so, however, would have reduced the organization's effectiveness in meeting its mission.

As co-manager of the program, NACo works with a volunteer advisory group to identify and evaluate the products offered and oversees the competitive bid process to select suppliers. (Vendors with connections to association leaders are excluded from consideration, and elected officials do not intrude on the competitive selection process.)

To market GPA, NACo partners with state associations of counties. In 2004 GPA registered more than $500 million in sales, with NACo estimating that local agencies saved approximately 20 percent on their purchases by using the program.

In addition, NACo offers a supplemental retirement program for county employees, debt-collection services, a human resources consulting service program for employment-related background checks, and a service for recovering insurance assets for environmental liabilities. "We try to find niches that aren't being met in the county marketplace," said a NACo employee. "We could make a lot of money selling affinity credit cards, but we don't do that because it doesn't benefit our constituency."

Similarly, a company once approached RSNA with the concept of a permanent, year-round exhibit of radiological equipment that would essentially take the place of RSNA's trade show. RSNA's board gave serious thought to going into business with the company, investing six months and $60,000 to research the proposal. But even after the company offered to double RSNA's payment, the association rejected the proposal. To the CEO, it was a simple call: "It clearly was not in our mission," he said.

For NACo, RSNA, and rest of the study group, the potential for profit is not a prerequisite when considering a product or service. That attitude does not prevail among the comparison group, where

> "AARP has over 36 million members, with thousands of volunteers and employees and strong offices in 53 states and territories. There is no other AARP, anywhere. We provide valuable information through community outreach, our publications, our website, advertising, and other channels. And we do the research that helps us listen to and understand our members. We advocate for causes—through regulation, legislation and litigation—that are important to our members and that enhance the public good. We are proudly, fiercely nonpartisan. Our collective purpose remains making life better for everyone as they age, helping people do what no individual can do alone."
>
> **– Bill Novelli, CEO, AARP**

we found several examples of associations that evaluated products and services based on the potential to generate net revenue.

In one case, an organization with declining dues revenue found itself on the verge of a financial crisis. In its search for options, the association discovered it could obtain federal grants to provide services to organizations in other countries. The influx of cash from these ventures solved the short-term financial crisis but created larger problems with members, who complained, legitimately, that the grant activity was not in line with the organization's mission.

Concentrating its efforts on an activity not related to its mission caused the organization to lose touch with the needs of members and to decrease services to them. Many members, presumably resenting this neglect, chose not to renew their memberships. In the end, the association's efforts did not prevent the financial crisis; they merely delayed it.

In another case, an association in the comparison group had a history of initiating programs that appeared to be good ideas from a financial standpoint but inevitably didn't hit the mark with either members' needs or the marketplace. Some, for example, were seen by state associations as directly competing for the same target market and thus became sources of tension. The programs' lack of success may have resulted from a deficient understanding of members and the marketplace.

During interviews, staff at this association acknowledged that, in their search for products and services, they always placed a priority on what will make money—and the more money, the better. Members' needs are almost an afterthought. Despite this financial orientation, the association still finds itself in a penny-pinching mode most years.

"There's a real sense here that the focus is just on high-revenue things," said one employee. "A lot of times [members] have ideas that are financially not feasible, but when we hear from them we try to make what we're doing meet their needs."

No fear of failure

To find the right mix of products and services that align with their missions, remarkable associations willingly engage in experimentation. They doggedly protect their core purpose and related activities while investigating new initiatives. What's more, they fully expect many of their efforts to fall flat. As one employee at NACo noted, "We think of programs as pancakes. You ought to be able to throw the first two away."

Far from being facetious, this employee was simply reflecting the cultural norms at NACo, where failures of products and services are not swept under the carpet. Instead, staff and volunteers openly analyze failures to extract lessons learned and identify possible ways to repurpose the information or the concept.

The willingness to experiment—and fail—in their quest to better serve members is evident throughout the study group. For the most part, interviewees from these remarkable associations spoke openly and candidly about the products and services that fell far short of expectations for whatever reason: failure to attract attendees, resonate with the majority of members, or generate revenue to sustain the venture. They also talked about the systems they have in place to evaluate and improve their offerings.

GO OR NO-GO

"This organization gives us permission to try something new and not succeed. They embrace good ideas and work on them."
— National Association of Counties

"So few things have been launched that it would be hard to have any flops."
— Matched pair comparison association

Remarkable associations do not believe in permanent pilot programs; they do not spend years trying to make a failed effort work. At AARP, an employee in the research department explained, "We have had our share of products that have not been successful from the start, but we change them based on our research and findings. We learn from mistakes. We either pull the product or restructure the product and launch it again."

RSNA also acknowledges that missteps occur, even though it follows an assessment process before giving the go-ahead to a new project or product. When asked how the association deals with product failures, one RSNA employee simply observed, "People talk about it and laugh and learn from it."

Employees at associations in the comparison group were rarely that forthcoming in interviews conducted by the research investigators. In addition to being reluctant to discuss product and program failures, they usually could not describe what the association learned or did differently as a result.

CHAPTER 4

Commitment to Analysis and Feedback

*Commitment to Analysis and Feedback:
Consistently exhibiting data-driven strategies
and dialogue and engagement, with a CEO
who serves as a broker of ideas.*

REMARKABLE ASSOCIATIONS make a practice of aligning their products and services with their mission and keeping members at the center of their universe. But how do they know whether they have hit the mark or missed by a mile? By asking over and over, again and again, in every conceivable way.

Associations in the study group were continually learning about the environment in which they and their members operate. They didn't restrict themselves to formal research—which all did and did well—but looked for every opportunity to hold conversations with members and encourage dialogue between staff and volunteers. Then they actually did something with the information they had gathered, such as modifying a product, introducing a new service, or initiating change through board dialogue and deliberation. We also found that the CEO played a crucial, if somewhat low-profile, role in making that something happen.

Data, Data, Data

Measure 3: Data-Driven Strategies

If there's one phrase that sets remarkable associations apart from their counterparts, it's "Data, data, data." They gather information, analyze it, and then use it to become even better. Research—whether quantitative or qualitative, formal or anecdotal—is always put to use, not put on the shelf.

The third measure, **data-driven strategies**, refers to a continuous loop that remarkable associations tend to exhibit: They continually track member needs and issues as well as the wider environment, then collectively analyze the data to reach a shared understanding through asking, "What do we now know? What are we going to do about it?" These associations then incorporate the findings into their strategic and operational planning.

But the data collection doesn't stop there. It continues through another methodical, disciplined cycle of gathering, analyzing, and making changes because of what was learned.

Girl Scouts of the USA (GSUSA), for instance, constantly researches the societal trends that affect and influence its reason for being: the girls. Some factfinding is done through the Girl Scout Research Institute, a separate entity that focuses on informed public policy making, and some projects, including data calibration with the U.S. Census office, through GSUSA's market research function.

"How are the needs and experiences of girls changing?" Every time GSUSA asks that question, it makes a commitment to seeing the world with new eyes. Results are communicated vertically and horizontally throughout the organization, at the national and local levels and to staff as well as volunteers. This leads to the development of contemporary programs that appeal to today's girls.

In recent years, GSUSA's data-driven strategies led to a series of initiatives aimed at helping girls develop math and financial literacy skills; a National Bone Health Campaign to prevent osteoporosis; Girls Go Tech, a mentoring partnership that links girls with female scientists; and an antiviolence education program. Also, by keeping a close watch on census data, GSUSA was able to respond early on, with targeted, bilingual materials and special programs, to an increase in Hispanic girls.

In contrast, a comparison association did not do the research that would have opened its leaders' eyes to coming population changes and their potential effect on the organization's traditional member-ship base. Because it was slow to develop programs aimed at anyone other than its traditional members, the organization has struggled with membership attrition as well as brand identity. It lost momen-tum by not researching environmental and membership trends and examining how to adapt while remaining true to its mission.

Beyond the formal market research or environmental scanning done by associations in the study group, we found a commitment to mining data from just about every encounter with members.

The staff and leaders at remarkable associations are constantly listening to members and sharing the information they glean from those contacts. Remarkable associations also face the facts: They're not so arrogant as to presume that they know better than what the data tell them. When new data demonstrate that the present course, no matter how well conceived, is in error, remarkable associations do not hesitate to make adjustments. An employee of the American College of Cardiology (ACC) put it this way: "We do market research, we do feasibility studies, because that way we can bring data to the board. We don't just run with something because it sounds like a great idea."

Integrated Systems

Here are additional data-driven examples culled from the study group:

- ACC has two groups that do environmental scanning. Each member of the internal (staff) group focuses on tracking trends in one of five major areas, such as demographics or economics, that ACC has deemed essential to its future. Members forming an external group periodically review the trend information to add insights from their perspectives. ACC's chapters also provide trend observations. All the results contribute to the development of annual initiatives and long-term strategic goals.

The executive committee, which also serves as the strategic planning committee, assigns several metrics, or key measures, to each of ACC's strategic goals. These key measures include statistical performance of publications and conferences (attendance, readership scores, abstract submissions), membership numbers (satisfaction scores, retention), customer service metrics (call center waiting times, Web access), and financial performance (revenue growth, revenue diversification). Each quarter, ACC's leaders evaluate the annual initiatives in view of the progress made on strategic goals and make adjustments as needed.

- In addition to ongoing focus groups and surveys, including consumer opinion polls, the American Dental Association (ADA) relies on its 11 councils to study and report on issues relating to a specific area of interest. Recommendations are forwarded to the board of trustees. Given its history of refining internal and volunteer structures to better align to strategic needs and opportunities, ADA seems to adapt its structure to fit needs rather than try to fit issues into its existing structure.

- The Society for Human Resource Management (SHRM) routinely conducts readership and advertising surveys, member needs assessments, member perception surveys, research about the workplace environment, and analyses of Web usage, as well as product evaluations and informal discussions with members.

SHRM also maintains a sophisticated database that enables it to track member activity. "We look at what books they are buying, what they are doing, what questions they are asking, what resources they use," said one staff member. "We analyze as much information as possible as a way of serving them better and understanding their needs."

• Associated General Contractors (AGC) posts surveys on its Web site that ask members a variety of questions about potential products and services: Are you interested in this product? How much would you pay for this service? What format would you prefer? Is this important for your business? The results are analyzed to determine the costs and time involved, whether an author or someone else is needed to develop the product, and a production timeline.

"We know who the product is for, who the market is, before production even begins," said one employee. "And the businesses that buy our products know we have done our research."

The Web-based surveys supplement formal research into member satisfaction and needs, environmental and competitive trends, and economic forecasting done by AGC's staff economist. All are part of AGC's disciplined approach to new initiatives, which includes earmarking a percentage of its annual marketing budget for business/product development. AGC also sets specific goals in this area (for example, "increase product line revenue by an average of 10 percent each year"). Over 10 years, such steps helped AGC reduce its dependence on membership dues as a part of total income by 26 percent.

♦ ♦ ♦ ♦ ♦ ♦
HOMEWORK VERSUS GUESSWORK

"We ask a lot of questions, through interactions with our members and staff and through research and surveys. That's how we learn more about our members."
– Society for Human Resource Management

"No, we don't do any formal scanning or research."
– Matched pair comparison association

We also noticed that employees at remarkable associations usually can clearly articulate who their competition is and often recite precise percentages of any membership overlap between their organization and the competition.

PUT TO THE TEST

AARP might well represent the gold standard for association research. Everything it does is driven by research, research, and more research. Much of the data gathering is designed and implemented by a 200-person research department, which focuses on three main areas: Medicare and health, marketing and membership, and environmental scanning of all types.

AARP conducts annual employee satisfaction surveys, employee exit interviews, member focus groups, telephone surveys, opinion polls, product evaluation surveys, and studies of ethnographics and econometrics. It tracks media coverage and the performance of its partnerships and affiliations. Through an outside call center, it keeps tabs on membership needs and interests, brand recognition, approval and product satisfaction ratings, and advocacy issues. AARP knows its members so well that it can tell you how often they take vacations, what airline they fly most frequently, and where they prefer to shop.

No product or service is released to the market without first undergoing an extensive, structured research process. As one employee explained, "We have learned not to act unless we are sure of the outcomes." The process typically includes a pilot test of both the product and its marketing, followed by an evaluative focus group. If something isn't quite right, AARP repackages or repositions the product and does additional market testing.

Relying on research-based information to guide strategic and tactical decisions at all levels has affected AARP both externally and internally. Noted one employee, "External changes include better member satisfaction and making the right decisions. For internal purposes, we look at ways to streamline processes and operating efficiencies. Employees and members are better satisfied, and the organization is better aligned with [its] strategic goals and objectives."

Given the research expertise it has developed, it's not surprising that AARP is now involved in a joint venture, a for-profit research company, that focuses on the population aged 50 and over.

The Ohio Society of CPAs (OSCPA) even has a group of members who volunteer to attend the courses offered by competitors and report on their experiences. "They tell us what they saw, the differences between our programs and others', and how we can be better or more effective," said one staff member.

In short, remarkable associations continuously and vigorously do their homework.

Ongoing Conversations

Measure 4: Dialogue and Engagement

Although remarkable associations have developed an expertise in gathering information, they know that's not enough. They also nurture a culture in which the information is analyzed and shared throughout the organization. Everyone, not just senior managers and elected leaders, is expected to use that data to figure out what actions the data are demanding of the organization.

The fourth measure, **dialogue and engagement**, is characterized by a close-knit, consistent culture where all employees not only receive the same script, in the form of the same information, but also see the potential to contribute to a blockbuster production. Whether they have lead or supporting roles or work behind the scenes is not relevant. Rather, they all share equally in the responsibility to contribute and add value to the association.

This culture is the natural outgrowth of what numerous interviewees described as "constant communication." Many within the study group would no doubt echo the employee at the Society for Human Resource Management (SHRM) who said, "We all discuss decisions openly with each other. We have a desire to collaborate with each other, and we do it in mission-driven ways.

"We aren't competitive here with each other," continued the same employee. "We are here to serve the same people and do what's best for the profession." That desire to always put the organization first, before individual or departmental gain, was displayed repeatedly in the study group.

Demolishing the Silos

Remarkable associations generally do not exhibit what's typically referred to as the silo mentality—organizational fragmentation by department or responsibility. When asked about signature products, for example, employees of great associations usually gave the same answers no matter what department they worked in or what their supervisory level. They shared a common view of who the association was and how well it served its members.

Contrast that clear understanding of organization identity and purpose with the confusion often displayed among employees of associations in the comparison group. It was common for staff in different departments to identify different signature products, usually the ones in their own area. At one association, for instance, a senior staff director said, "[The association]'s signature products and services and the ones in my area are very different." Another employee at the same association responded, "The signature products and services are different depending on whether you classify them by revenue or by the customer."

Remarkable associations avoid this type of segregation. For them, everything is about members. Therefore, they ensure internal dialogue continually takes place throughout the organization about its direction, priorities, and reason for being (serving members). Here are some examples of how they do that:

- Within five weeks of their starting date, new employees of OSCPA meet with the CEO, who explains the organization's vision and goals. Periodically, the entire staff assembles for a review of OSCPA's annual goals and a progress report.

- The National Association of Counties (NACo) regularly holds "County 101" sessions with its national staff (and vendor members, too, if requested) to help ensure that everyone is clear about what its members do.

  To emphasize the importance of information sharing throughout the organization, NACo holds weekly meetings in which staff are expected to talk to one another about how their various areas intersect and interact. It also holds cross-functional team retreats to ensure activities not only align with the strategic plan but also complement one another.

  "We've gotten rid of the silo mentality internally," explained one director. "Every department used to operate so autonomously that there wasn't a working relationship between any of them. Now, we coordinate efforts."

• As at many associations, SHRM's employees gather once a month to welcome new hires and celebrate employment anniversaries, but they also hear an update about the state of the association. During this all-staff meeting, the CEO reviews overall goals and discusses what SHRM is doing as an organization to meet those goals.

Thanks to such ongoing dialogues, staff members at remarkable associations not only understand their own roles but also understand

---

EVERYONE AT THE TABLE

By all accounts, the board and staff of the American College of Cardiology (ACC) have always had a solid, respectful relationship. "What has changed is what the staff can contribute and it's no longer just the logistics of organizational arrangements," reported one long-time employee. "Now there's more of a partnership between staff and the board in terms of feedback about the marketplace. Staff focus on how we can give the board the data they need to set direction. The board still makes the decisions but asks more for [our] opinions and input."

The change was made consciously by a CEO and an elected president who wanted to increase board effectiveness. In addition to clarifying board and staff roles, they revamped the physical layout used for board meetings. In the past, the 30-member board would sit, in alphabetical order, around a square table. The elected president sat at the head of the table, marked by the presence of a lectern. Participation was somewhat perfunctory, with most board members simply sitting at the table and reading reports. The arrangement relegated senior staff to the perimeter of the room; if called on to speak, they had to walk up to the lectern.

Now, with no designated head of the table, the elected president, CEO, and staff vice presidents sit among the rest of the board members, who are no longer assigned seats. The tenor of the board meetings changed, along with the physical arrangements. Board members became more engaged with one another and with staff and are more inclined to spend their time synthesizing information rather than reading staff reports.

"The meetings are much more interesting, with people asking more questions," added the employee. "The board is thinking broader about strategy and decisions for the whole organization."

and appreciate the roles of their colleagues. All employees share a strong commitment to the notion that "We are here for the members." Departmental boundaries and petty turf wars give way to a shared drive to deliver high quality products and services that address member needs and deliver on the mission.

Moreover, remarkable associations effectively maintain a class-less structure. Rather than focusing on distinctions between executive and staff or profit centers and service areas, these organizations reflect a neighborhood culture characterized by shared values and a unified purpose.

SEEKING ANSWERS AT ALL LEVELS

"What can I do to help Girl Scouting be the best personal leadership development program for girls ages 5-17?"

That's the question GSUSA has put to all its constituents in order to develop its Core Business Strategy, which is intended to ensure the organization's future success and growth. Work began in 2004, with the Core Business Strategy scheduled to be fully operational by the organization's 100th anniversary in 2012.

To encourage dialogue among its members, GSUSA set up a special Web site and e-mail link related to the Core Business Strategy and invited them to "be willing to do things differently and strive to makes the changes that will result in the future we seek." At the same time, members are reassured, "[The Girl Scout Promise and Law] are tied to the rich history of Girl Scouts and they will continue to be at the heart of the Girl Scout experience."

At its triennial convention, GSUSA hosted an "open space conversation" and numerous "strategy cafés." In the former, national delegates working in groups devoted a day to discussing one question: "What would our governance structure look like on a national and local level if it met the test of being efficient, decisive, and action-oriented?" If interested, delegates could also participate in the strategy cafés, small-group discussions focused on one of five strategic priorities or the Girl Scout culture.

All member feedback is funneled through six strategic teams—Program Model and Pathways, Volunteerism, Brand, Funding, Organizational Structure and Governance, and Culture. Each team includes members from all organizational levels, functions, and geographic regions.

The Great Go-Between

Measure 5: CEO as a Broker of Ideas

No matter how good the script, an interactive dialogue among all the players is unlikely to occur without a director—in this case, the association's chief executive officer. The association leader must not only understand the organization's vision but also be able to engage others in defining, refining, and responding to that vision and all it entails.

While CEOs may certainly be visionary leaders, what's more important is their ability to facilitate visionary thinking throughout the organization. What sets the study group apart from the comparison group is the fifth measure of success: **the CEO as a broker of ideas**.

To CEOs of remarkable associations, what matters is not their vision for the association but rather the members' vision. To be sure, the CEO plays a key role in creating a vision for the organization. That role, however, rests with gathering consensus around a member-generated vision rather than forcing buy-in into a personal vision.

All the associations that participated in the study, no matter which research group they were in, had transitioned away from an autocratic, controlling CEO at some point in the preceding 20 years. Stories were told of former CEOs who edited every communication sent by the association, pitted department directors against one another in mean-spirited competition, played favorites among staff and members, and even hand-picked which flowers to plant at the association's headquarters. Those days are gone, although not necessarily long gone.

Virtually all the CEOs whose associations participated in the Measures project were described as fostering a "team" or "family" environment within the association and as being willing to listen to others' ideas. Yet having the ability to listen and be open to others' ideas isn't enough. The CEO must also stimulate energy and engagement among and between staff and volunteers and must be willing to step aside at times to facilitate a discussion of ideas without dictating an outcome.

In remarkable associations, the CEO helps both elected leaders and staff think in terms of what is possible and enables things to happen rather than decreeing what will happen. Staff input is both welcomed and respected, with no apparent class distinctions giving more weight to some employees' ideas over others'.

A MODEL OF COLLABORATION

At Associated General Contractors (AGC), management doesn't just talk about the importance of working as a team. They also model the behavior through a unique "shared responsibility" arrangement between the CEO and COO.

Both positions report directly to the board, are similarly compensated, and have equal standing in the eyes of members and staff. The difference is that the CEO focuses primarily on external affairs while the COO concentrates on internal operations. The two leaders, whom the board hired as a team following the short tenure of the previous CEO, describe their roles as "business partners." Staff are not confused by the unusual leadership structure but see it as a model for collaborative decision making throughout the organization.

An example from the comparison group helps put this measure in context. One association made a concerted effort to dismantle a longstanding bureaucracy in which ideas had to work their way up through the chain of command. Many ideas died along the way, which had dampened further creativity. Despite the introduction of cross-functional teams, however, staff continued to believe that senior managers would block innovations, so they took new ideas directly to the CEO.

Rather than open an organizational dialogue, the CEO primarily communicated with the employee or member who had brought forward the idea, bypassing input from other staff and members. As a result, the CEO actually undermined any efforts to foster innovation and teamwork. Distrust among staff and departments was the norm—to the point where employees were reluctant to attend meetings on other departments' "turf"—so sharing ideas did not occur easily. Perhaps not surprisingly, the association introduced few new products and services.

In this association, as in several other comparison associations, the CEO seemed isolated and had a different view of the organizational culture than most of the employees who were interviewed. In contrast, CEOs in the study group generally avoided being isolated by themselves, with senior staff, or with a group of elected officers. They took pains to clarify the roles and responsibilities expected of everyone—board, staff, and CEO—in the association partnership.

CHAPTER 5

Commitment to Action

*Commitment to Action:
Consistently exhibiting organizational
adaptability and alliance building.*

T EXTBOOK STRATEGIC plans—complete with clearly outlined goals, objectives, and strategies that were reviewed and adjusted on a consistent basis—were present in many of the associations that participated in the Measures study. Interestingly, these were most common in the *comparison* group.

That's not to say that the associations in the study group are not strategic in determining who they are or where they are headed. On the contrary, as underscored in Chapters 3 and 4, remarkable associations never look away from their members. They amass data, engage in ongoing dialogues, and design products and services to support and serve those members. Make no mistake: These associations are truly strategic. All of them depend on a strategic plan, although theirs are often less formal than the plans of the comparison associations.

The difference is that remarkable associations don't just emphasize thinking strategically. They find it equally important to *act* strategically; they consistently implement their priorities. Associations in the study group may not have had as well-crafted or well-documented plans, but everyone—volunteers and staff alike—understood what the plan and goals were and lived them.

The comprehensive strategic plans of associations in the comparison group, in contrast, often ran contrary to their eventual actions or inactions. They often fail to act in ways that advance their strategic priorities. That is, their magnificently crafted, comprehensive strategic plans may result in little real change in the organization or the extent to which it serves its members. Similarly, several comparison associations frequently revised their strategic plans, yet little about the organization actually changed.

In other words, among remarkable associations, it matters what you do, not just what you say.

"We are not a sitting-still organization but an action organization." This statement, spoken by an employee of the SHRM, reflects the mindset of the study organizations.

The Will To Act

Measure 6: Organizational Adaptability

Most of the participating associations experienced at least one crisis during the 15-year study period, typically a financial setback or a leadership void. The comparison organizations tended to react more slowly than the study organizations. It seemed to take them longer not only to understand what was happening but also to determine the best course of action. A frequent response was to continue what they were already doing; they simply worked harder or more intensely, hoping the extra effort would resolve the crisis.

Remarkable associations demonstrated the sixth measure, **organizational adaptability,** by not only weathering crises but also learning from them. In the face of markedly declining membership or program revenue, for example, study organizations quickly assessed the situation and then took action—with no excuses.

The economic slowdown of the early 1990s certainly affected Associated General Contractors (AGC), which registered its highest rate of membership attrition in 1992. AGC realized that it could no longer afford to maintain its staffing levels or its headquarters building and lost no time in making the tough, but necessary, calls. In addition to making staff cutbacks, it sold the building—not a highly popular decision—and relocated to rented quarters for more than a decade.

At one time, the National Association of Counties (NACo) found itself in a deficit situation. In one year, it cut a $2.5 million deficit by $900,000 by taking decisive action. NACo instituted a hiring freeze, slashed staff travel, and cut other expenditures across the board. "We started right away, which is why we were able to pay off the debt," recalled one employee.

Both AGC and NACo moved quickly to recover from their financial challenges. In both associations, these financial crises have had the lasting effect of instilling more discipline within the budgeting and planning processes. Both have made a commitment to avoiding such situations in the future. NACo consciously budgets at least 4 percent of its annual revenues to reserves, to ensure a financial cushion.

NACo also revamped its budgeting process to increase board ownership of the organization's fiscal health. Although NACo staff prepare the budget, members of the executive, finance, and auditing committees review it during a special meeting. "They get a very detailed picture of what we're spending money on, and they can ask any questions they'd like," explained one employee. "We also talk about salaries and discuss any trends. We involve them as much as possible, so the board isn't just getting a budget handed to them by staff."

To lessen the likelihood of experiencing a financial crisis again, AGC made a commitment to decreasing its dependency on dues income. Its eventual aim is to have 50 percent of its income from nondues sources. Each year has brought AGC closer to that goal. Some of that progress may be attributed to the articulation of specific goals, such as "eliminate management conference programs that continue to operate at a loss by FY06."

Prune to Grow

AGC is not alone in its determination to terminate programs that do not contribute to its mission. Most associations within the study group exhibited the same behavior. To them, all programs and activities are subject to scrutiny. Nothing is considered an entitlement or a sacred cow whose worth goes unquestioned.

Some examples from the study associations illustrate this point:

- Several years ago, the Ohio Society of CPAs (OSCPA) made a significant organizational change. The society's board voted to eliminate its chapters, thus creating one state level of dues.

This decision, recommended by two grassroots task forces, was based on the belief that the chapter structure did not contribute member value and detracted from OSCPA's ability to provide core services. Dissolving the chapters gave OSCPA direct access to all of its members and provided more direct communication and delivery of services. Although controversial, this decision has come to be accepted as the right thing to do among the majority of OSCPA members.

- SHRM engages in what the author Peter Drucker referred to as "purposeful abandonment." Each year, teams of staff members present their evaluations of existing and proposed products and services. Programs or services that are judged to no longer meet the needs of members are either revised or dropped and replaced with something new.

"A lot of what we do is growth through selected mutation. Sometimes products are reinvented to adapt to new changes," explained one employee. One instance is *HR News*, SHRM's former print newspaper, which was transformed into the news section on SHRM's Web site. The society maintains its commitment to delivering news but found a better way to do it.

SHRM also changed its board selection process as part of its focus on continuous improvement. As the organization continued to grow and change, SHRM needed specific skills and competencies on its board to ensure the growth continued.

In the past, SHRM volunteers worked in volunteer capacities that were progressively larger or more national in scope before becoming board members. Today, SHRM members apply to be on the board of directors, submitting resumes and going through interviews, a process much like the one members themselves use on the job. "Board members are chosen based on their skills and qualifications and how well they meet certain criteria," explained one staff member.

- Every time they attend a management retreat, NACo's senior staff devotes half a day to talking about which programs they should introduce, what they should modify or adapt in some way, and what they should stop doing completely. Staff then look to members to validate their recommendations, by comparing the three lists to data gathered through membership surveys and other research vehicles.

Mission Sensitive

As willing as they are to change, remarkable associations know what *not* to change. Their mission and purpose remain the touchstones. They understand that what is needed to serve their core purpose changes as the environment in which they operate changes.

Girl Scouts of the USA (GSUSA) has never veered away from its mission to serve girls. But GSUSA *has* changed the wording of its bedrock Promise and Law, the way it communicates with girls (the Internet is the preferred method today), the methods used to deliver the Girl Scout program (not just traditional troops), and its uniforms (numerous redesigns to stay contemporary), to name a few examples.

The Brownie uniform worn in 2006 certainly looks different from the one worn in 1956 or even 1996, but what that uniform represents hasn't changed. GSUSA, like most of the study associations, constantly engages in the balancing act of remaining true to its mission while investigating and implementing adaptations to its operations and services. The organization values its history and tradition but acknowledges that what worked yesterday is not always relevant to what will work today.

Surprisingly, we found no distinction between proactive and reactive change among the associations studied. Our data confirm that no organization—regardless of how remarkable it is—can predict change with full accuracy and therefore be on target with its response in all instances. From time to time, all organizations are caught off guard and must react to unplanned events (such as the terrorist attacks on the United States on September 11, 2001).

The type of change is not as significant as how the organization responds to and learns from the change. Our data indicate that remarkable associations do not panic. Whether or not the change is anticipated, they maintain a clear understanding of their core purpose and willingly adapt how they do business to remain consistent with that purpose. They remain steadfast in their commitment to their members and their mission, often avoiding changes that have the potential to shift them away from that core, even if by doing so they sacrifice immediate payoffs.

REVISITING THE PAST—OR LIVING IN IT

"Programs are very easy to add, but they're hard to get out of. So three years down the road, if we're still doing it, people ask, 'Why?'"

– National Association of Counties

"Generally, we do the same products and services we've done for a long time... This organization protects the status quo. It doesn't like to change much."

– Matched pair comparison association

Partnering for the Right Purpose

Measure 7: Alliance Building

Forming alliances with other organizations—whether nonprofit, for-profit, or government—was high on the priority list for both the study and comparison associations. Most of them had built several alliances that proved effective in generating revenue, raising awareness around a key issue, or building their organizational brand.

Where the two research groups differ is how they approach the seventh measure, **alliance building.** Associations in the study group pursue alliances that relate to existing strategies or that form a tight fit with their mission and purpose. In that regard, they determine with whom *not* to partner as much as with whom they should partner.

While remarkable associations are willing to admit they can't do everything on their own, they bring self-confidence to their alliance-building activities. Secure in who they are and what they bring to the table, these associations communicate clear expectations for each specific partnership and do not hesitate to walk away if a win-win situation does not materialize. But they're also willing to admit what they can't do on their own.

GSUSA, for example, aggressively searches for other organizations that have the expertise, skills, credibility, contacts, and other resources that complement or augment its own resources. Alliance building is all about getting the job done for the girls. GSUSA has collaborated with VISA to provide money management resources geared to preteens and teenagers, with the Environmental Protection Agency to develop an environmental health badge and "My Planet" online games for its Web site, with the Lucent Technologies Foundation to encourage minority girls to pursue careers in math and science, and with the Ad Council of America to produce a public service campaign aimed at building girls' interest in math and technology. These represent just a few of GSUSA's many collaborations.

In contrast, its matched-pair comparison association typically approaches alliances as a means of paying the bills (corporate sponsorships) rather than as an opportunity to expand mission-based programming. Not surprisingly, the comparison association has far fewer alliances.

The American Dental Association (ADA) saw a need among its members for more sophisticated practice-management knowledge. Recognizing its limitations in that area, ADA turned to Northwestern University's Kellogg School of Management to develop a mini-MBA program specifically for dentists.

In that same vein, NACo collaborated with the Wagner Graduate School of Public Service at New York University to develop a county leadership institute. NACo asks state associations to identify up-and-coming leaders to participate in the four-day program. Corporate partners who underwrite portions of the program benefit from added visibility with this constituency.

ADA also sees the potential for collaboration with its competitors at state and local levels. It invested in the development of the

---

FINDING THE COMMON GROUND

In one recent year, the National Association of Counties (NACo) collaborated with approximately 30 organizations ranging from the Smart Growth Network to the National Animal Control Association. One collaboration goes much farther back, to the 1980s. That's when NACo and six associations with similar interests and overlapping issues formed The Big 7.

Other members of The Big 7 include the U.S. Conference of Mayors, National League of Cities, National Governors Association, National Conference of State Legislatures to name a few—several of which NACo considers competition for some of its products and services. But any competition takes a back seat when representatives of The Big 7 meet monthly. They discuss hot issues and emerging trends and identify opportunities for working together and potentially pooling resources to advance a common cause. Every two years, the chair of the group rotates among the seven associations.

Tripartite System, a software package for managing and sharing membership data across a common platform. More than 60 state and local dental societies use the system to support membership billing, patient referrals, information retrieval, mailing list management, and grassroots lobbying efforts.

Whether forging alliances or remaking themselves, remarkable associations do not stray from clearly stated goals and they maintain a disciplined process to achieve those goals. Their counterparts in the comparison group are more likely to seize on opportunities that offer the potential for short-term gain. In general, they seem less concerned about the long-term implications of their actions.

CHAPTER 6

Old Saws and Fresh Cuts

IN WHAT ways, if any, do the study's findings challenge the conventional wisdom?

That question, which Jim Collins posed to the Measures of Success Task Force, proved as intriguing as identifying the seven factors that distinguish remarkable associations from the rest of the pack.

To answer the question, we needed to identify what constituted conventional wisdom within the field of association management. First individually, then as a group, the task force compiled a list of widely held beliefs prevalent in the profession. Next we systematically compared the findings to conventional wisdom, acknowledging that it is far easier to disprove something than to prove it.

For example, consider the statement, "All apples are red." While proving this statement would pose quite a challenge, disproving it would not: you'd simply have to find one yellow apple.

In some instances, we easily picked out the yellow apples—that is, the remarkable associations did not adhere to conventional wisdom

PUT TO THE TEST

The Measures Task Force compiled these statements of conventional wisdom within the association management profession, then tested them against the data gathered in the matched-pair research study.

1. One person should be at the top.
2. Keep 50 percent of annual expenses in reserves.
3. CEO should be an association professional.
4. CEO should come from outside the organization rather than within.
5. Don't get too far ahead of the membership.
6. Elections should reflect the democratic process.
7. Elected leaders should move through the ranks.
8. Small boards are better than big boards.
9. Organizations should be more member-driven than staff-driven.
10. Be innovative/on the cutting edge.
11. Run the association like a corporation.
12. Engage in consensus decision making.
13. Participatory management is best.
14. CEO should take a back seat to the elected leader.
15. CEO is always right.
16. Have a one-year term for elected leaders.
17. Association activities require constituent buy-in.
18. Radical times require radical change.
19. Proactive change is better than reactive change.
20. The board sets the policy; the staff implements it.
21. Staff should not be involved in selection of leaders.
22. CEO has no vote on the board.
23. Have a strategic plan.
24. A higher market share is better.

yet they consistently flourished. The following are the conventional beliefs not supported by this study:

The smaller the board, the better. Were this conventional wisdom true, we should have seen smaller boards among the study group and larger boards in the comparison group. This was not the case. In fact, in one instance, a study association *added* two seats to its board, following a governance review.

Within the study group, board size ranged from eight (Radiological Society of North America) to 40 (Girl Scouts of the USA). The size of GSUSA's board does not hinder the organization's efficiency, speed of action, or ability to maintain focus on its mission. Study organizations with larger boards (more than 20 members) developed systems and structures that disperse power and decision-making authority.

Our data indicate board size isn't a significant factor in the effectiveness of the organization. What *does* matter is how boards and staff understand and align their roles. In general, boards in the study organizations were more strategic than operational. Similarly, study organizations were committed to collecting and analyzing data, which likely facilitated strategic decision making.

Board members should be selected via a democratic process. Many associations view elections as a reflection of democratic culture and values. Several organizations in both the study and comparison groups used the "any member can run for the board" approach.

Others relied on a nominating committee to select an essentially uncontested slate with one candidate for each open position. Two out of the nine study associations use a competency model in which board candidates are selected based upon their skills, knowledge, and experience; one of those associations has even considered hiring a search firm to identify viable candidates.

Although the study associations value previous leadership experience, none requires volunteers to follow a rigid, up-the-ladder approach to board service.

Associations in the study group do not favor a particular selection or election process to populate their boards. There is, however, a common denominator among remarkable associations. They are highly effective in maintaining transparency and communicating how the process for identifying and recruiting capable, credible, and competent leaders works.

The CEO should be an association professional and come from outside the organization and its membership. The data do not support this assertion. Only three of the nine associations in the study group followed this model when selecting their current CEO. Two associations had selected their current CEO from within the membership, and four had chosen an internal candidate. Interestingly, two of the latter group had turned to the internal candidate after the short tenure of a CEO from the outside.

Regardless of their background or how they came to the position, CEOs of remarkable associations typically had one trait in common: They matched themselves to the personality of the organization and understood what it expected of them.

Proactive change is better. Conventional wisdom would have us believe that remarkable associations take a proactive stance toward change, rather than a reactive one, yet that distinction did not emerge from the data. In fact, the type of change is not as significant as the response it evokes from the organization. Whether they initiate change themselves or react to change, remarkable associations do what it takes to remain committed to their core purpose. They not only learn from the change but also exhibit the will to take the action it requires of them.

Reserves should equal 50 percent of annual expenses. Study findings revise this statement upward. Most associations in the study group have reserves of approximately 75 percent of their annual expenses. At least three of them have drawn on their reserves to invest in programs or organizational improvements to benefit members but still maintained a comfortable financial cushion.

Remarkable associations see "nonprofit" as a tax status, not a mental state. They understand that both for-profits and nonprofits make money; the difference lies in what is done with those profits. For-profit companies pay dividends to their shareholders, while nonprofits reinvest retained earnings into member programs and services.

Taking a for-profit company's perspective, members would be viewed as a market, triggering the question, "What can we sell to them?" Instead, remarkable associations view members as drivers, and the question becomes, "How can we serve them, and what do they need?"

WHO'S DRIVING?

Association executives are often asked to characterize their organizations as being either member-driven or staff-driven. Conventional wisdom says it's better to have volunteer leaders guide and remain in control of decision making (member-driven). Or, depending on whom you ask, some people argue that the best choice is to be "balanced-driven." In that model, neither staff nor members dominate decision making; decisions are reached through the cooperative efforts of both groups.

Our data do not indicate a relationship between decision-making models and organizational success. No one model predominates among the study or comparison groups. We found just as many member-driven associations among the comparison group as staff-driven associations among the study group. Some could also be described as balanced.

That said, the remarkable associations did differentiate themselves in a way that should put an end to the staff- versus member-driven debate. In short, the distinction doesn't matter. What *does* matter is being *data*-driven as well as *member-focused*.

Remarkable associations have a customer/member-service orientation; continually gather and analyze data about members and the external environment; and use their mission, which is all about the members, as the touchstone for all activities. The member-focused, data-driven model produces the best possible scenario: Staff drives achievement, but both member leaders and the staff ultimately achieve success by maintaining a well-informed focus on the members.

Comparing the Findings

We initially decided to apply Collins' methodology to associations because we had confidence in the matched-pair approach. We suspected that many of his findings from the for-profit sector would apply equally well to the association environment, assuming they withstood the test of a full-fledged, comprehensive study.

With our own findings now in hand, it's useful to see how they compare with some of Collins' concepts from the for-profit sector.

Profit is one means of measuring success, not *the* means. *Good to Great* reveals that great for-profit companies do not focus on their profits as an end; they have other ways of measuring their ability to deliver on their value proposition.

The same holds true for associations. Remarkable associations consistently achieve a positive bottom line. They do so by steadfastly focusing on members' needs and ensuring that they deliver quality products and services to meet those needs. Comparison organizations more typically made decisions based primarily, if not solely, on profit. Ironically, they did not necessarily perform in the black consistently and often experienced a greater rate of member attrition.

Remarkable associations never disregard profit. Rather, they focus on carefully documenting member needs and then deliberately and consistently fulfilling those needs. Their healthy bottom line is a rewarding byproduct of their efforts.

Focus on the core, and experiment around the fringes. The behavior of remarkable associations fully supports this concept. Remarkable associations never forget mission or members—why they were formed or who they serve—and are willing to undertake significant risks outside this core. In contrast, many organizations in the comparison group experienced changes that pulled them away from, or at least blurred, their mission.

Have a Big Hairy Audacious Goal (BHAG). Introduced in *Built to Last*, BHAG refers to a clear, compelling, and unifying focal point of effort for an organization. While remarkable associations had clearly stated goals and objectives, we did not find any evidence that they developed and pursued BHAGs. Their objectives flowed logically from their mission; as their mission remained constant, so, for the most part, did their objectives.

Foster a cultlike culture. Although the cultures of great companies are diverse, they share the characteristic of not accommodating the gadfly. Either people fit into the corporate mold or they move on.

Cultures of remarkable associations were typically described as "familylike" by those working within them; "cultlike" did not seem to apply. Remarkable associations had strong member-focused cultures. Staff members are never ambiguous about why they come to work each day: to serve the members. Moreover, they take pride and joy in doing so.

Exhibit Level 5 leadership. In *Good to Great*, Collins coined the expression "Level 5 Leader" to describe a CEO who exhibits personal humility as well as professional resolve. He found, much to his surprise, that great companies were led by people who were often socially shy, self-effacing, and reserved. Collins noted, "They are more like Lincoln and Socrates than Patton or Caesar."

We found that most associations, both study and comparison, had had their share of Pattons and Caesars during the study period—although usually not in recent years—and had thrived nonetheless. Given the wide range of leadership styles and personalities among CEOs past and present, we did not have evidence to suggest that Level 5 leaders are necessary for associations to function in a consistently remarkable way.

We did confirm that the study organizations were led by highly effective individuals who shared several characteristics. CEOs of remarkable associations understand the importance of including both members and staff in ongoing dialogues. Although they did not manage by consensus per se, they did ensure that they gathered input from a variety of sources before making decisions.

Moreover, these CEOs understand and are comfortable with their role as a steward—not owner—of the association. The association belongs to the members, so its vision must emanate from them, not from the CEO's corner office or from a small group of leaders.

Be a legislative leader. Collins' 2005 monograph, *Good to Great and the Social Sectors,* advances the notion that CEOs in the for-profit sector have "executive" skills while those in the social sector have "legislative" skills. Specifically, the latter group relies on "persuasion, political currency, and shared interests to create conditions for the right decisions to happen."

Our research partially supports Collins' hypothesis. Corporate executives may be hired for their vision; CEOs of remarkable associations are hired to facilitate visionary thinking and to create a culture of possibilities. They are rarely, if ever, the sole decision maker; they must share that responsibility with volunteer leaders, who rely on input from members and the environment. The findings emphasize that association CEOs are brokers, not sole proprietors, of ideas.

Get the right people on the bus and the wrong people off. This concept poses a challenge for associations because they have two sets of passengers—staff and volunteers. CEOs can exert much more influence with the former group than with the latter. Several CEOs in the study group spoke about making staff changes to improve performance and morale, while acknowledging that they can inherit volunteer leaders who make it challenging to forge effective partnerships between staff and volunteers.

Develop a "stop doing" list. *Good to Great* emphasizes that great organizations exercise the discipline to simply stop engaging in unproductive or inefficient activities. Likewise, remarkable associations maintain clear goals and have a disciplined process to evaluate how well their products and services remain aligned with their mission and members' documented needs. When a program or service no longer fits, these associations terminate it to make room for something better.

THE RESULTS IN CONTEXT

Findings from the Measures project, as well as the findings of Collins, are consistent with literature about learning organizations and systems. To use Collins' terminology, great organizations "build clocks rather than tell time." In other words, they build systems that effectively integrate inputs, processes, and outputs. Acting together, these various parts produce more than they could individually.

In *The Fifth Discipline Fieldbook* (1994, Doubleday), Peter M. Senge, Art Kleiner, Charlotte Roberts, Richard Ross, and Bryan Smith define a learning organization as one that transforms "experience into knowledge—accessible to the whole organization and relevant to its core purpose." Further, the authors observe that learning organizations:

Continuously test their experience. They compare what they think they know to the reality as derived from research.

Produce knowledge. In this context, knowledge means know-how. It is fundamentally different from information, which is data that knowledge transforms into effective action. The purpose of knowledge is not to merely inform but to change behavior.

Share knowledge. Knowledge is accessible to individuals throughout the organization.

Make learning relevant. Learning organizations gather knowledge that helps them forward their mission. They purposely focus on their core mission and don't become distracted by information overload.

These characteristics describe remarkable organizations as well. The Measures study revealed that disciplined organizations transform information they experience into knowledge (know-how) they can use to further their mission. They are in a constant quest for improvement.

A number of our findings are consistent with those identified by Collins. Several findings unique to the association environment are also evident. First, remarkable associations are intensely data-driven. They rarely miss an opportunity to solicit feedback, gather opinions, and collect statistics, all of which they analyze and act on. A second unique finding was the commitment by remarkable associations to ongoing dialogue and engagement, both among and between staff and volunteers.

The concept of collaborating for the right purpose does not have a counterpart in the corporate world. Unlike for-profit companies that engage in intense competition, associations seek to achieve their goals through cooperation, even if their collaborators pose competition in some areas. Few associations have the resources to accomplish all their goals on their own, so they must work with others in pursuit of fulfilling their mission.

The Road to Remarkable

In their own right, the seven measures of success are not groundbreaking concepts. After all, many associations form alliances and foster dialogue among and with their members.

Taken together, however, the seven measures overlap and interact in so many ways that they weave a pattern of long-term success for the associations that employ them to their fullest potential.

What truly distinguished associations in the study group was their performance relative to the seven measures: They exhibited them consistently and continually, integrating the measures into the way they did business and into their very culture.

Remarkable associations find it second nature to deliver stellar customer service; develop products, services, and alliances that support their mission and purpose; gather member data; and make the adaptations or clear-cut changes that enable them to continue fulfilling their mission to serve members. One measure feeds into another and yet another, as illustrated below.

Input and Output Framework

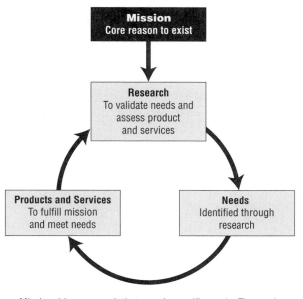

Mission drives research that reveals specific needs. The needs determine program, product, and service development, which are further evaluated to determine value.

Mission is subdivided into needs (identified through research) resulting in the development of products/services, which are then subjected to further research to see what is working and what needs to change.

When we looked at the mountains of printed material, pages of statistics, and transcripts of personal interviews, several general themes emerged. Overall, we observed that:

- **Members and mission are at the heart of remarkable associations—and member value is the blood that keeps the heart pumping.** While seeking to build and maintain a strong relationship with their members, remarkable organizations never stop being inquisitive about how they can refine and enhance the value they provide.

- **Remarkable associations deliver.** They continually research member needs; relate those needs to the mission; and then develop, adapt, and refine products and services. They always look for the best solutions to provide valuable resources and services.

- **All organizations must deal with setbacks, failures, and crises, but not all of them learn from these events.** The remarkable ones don't become frozen in place or time. They acknowledge their failures, learn from their experiences, make changes or adaptations, and move on.

We also noted these specific behaviors, which build on and add nuance to the seven measures outlined in Chapters 3, 4, and 5.

REMARKABLE ASSOCIATIONS...	GOOD ASSOCIATIONS OFTEN...
Have confidence in who they are and are well on the way to determining—or already know—who they want to be.	May still be struggling with who they are and have given little serious thought to who they want to be.
Ask what members need.	Decide what members need.
Do what needs to be done.	Talk about what needs to be done.
Have learned to let go of programs and services that no longer serve or resonate with members.	Continue to hang on to what may have worked in the past but may now be irrelevant.
Embrace product failures as an opportunity to learn how to better serve members; look for ways to re-use or repackage what failed.	View failures almost as embarrassments, as something not to revisit or even recall.
Enjoy camaraderie within an open, sharing environment where a sense of single purpose prevails. ("We're all in this together.")	May have a sense of teamwork within departments but usually not across the entire organization, leading to a silo mentality. ("That's not my job.")
Question the status quo.	Protect the status quo.

REMARKABLE ASSOCIATIONS...	GOOD ASSOCIATIONS OFTEN...
Are methodical and disciplined about collecting member data and opinions.	Take a random, inconsistent approach to gathering member data.
Use data vertically and horizontally, so it permeates the organization.	Use data vertically (usually a top-down approach).
Do their homework, through surveys, assessments, and evaluations, before launching or discontinuing a product or service.	Rely more on intuition, assumptions, and chance to guide product development and improvement.
Exhibit a "What if...?" mentality when confronting challenges.	Exhibit a "Yes, but..." mentality when challenges arise.
Remain attuned to the external environment, particularly the competition.	Do not engage in much scanning of the external environment; often rely on organizational leaders for view of the world.
Strive to understand what precipitated a crisis and face it head-on.	Make excuses or place blame when a crisis arises, often becoming immobilized by it.
Talk *with* members at every opportunity.	Talk *to* members, both in face-to-face and other types of communication.

One might be tempted to point to the list of associations in the study group and say, "Well, of course they can afford to do that because they have money/clout/fill in the blank." The fact is, all the study organizations have, at times during the study period, operated with severely limiting factors, including a large deficit, a serious IRS challenge, a sizeable decline in membership, the sudden death of a CEO, and a crisis within the members' profession. Those in the comparison group became paralyzed by such circumstances, often for years. They obsessed on their limitations and sought excuses for their inaction or inability to capitalize on opportunities.

In contrast, the remarkable associations not only recognize their limiting factors but also accept them as givens. Embracing the culture of opportunity as presented to them, they proceed to operate and accomplish their mission undeterred.

CEO CONFIDENTIAL

Data from the Measures of Success project could not prove exactly what is required to become a remarkable association. But the data did lead to the discovery of some practices that distinguish remarkable associations from their good counterparts.

If an association follows these practices, it will increase the probability that it, too, will become remarkable:

- **Keep your eyes and your minds wide open.** Products and services should emanate from two sources: your mission and members' documented needs.

- **Develop and foster a strong customer service culture.** Keeping members front and center is everyone's job.

- **Keep your balance.** Remain firm about the *what*—your mission—and flexible about the *how*—your products and services.

- **Clean your plate.** As you add new programs and services, eliminate those that no longer serve a need. Have only one sacred cow—your mission.

- **Seek to influence, not control.** The CEO's job is to facilitate visionary thinking and be a broker of ideas, not force others to adopt his or her vision.

- **Remain humble.** You don't know it all. The best source of what members need is the members themselves. Seek out their views often and in a variety of ways.

- **Be a good neighbor.** Seek out and foster relationships with organizations that may not share your overall mission but do share your desire to accomplish certain goals. Don't make friends for the sake of appearances or profits—do it for the sake of your mission.

Vital Statistics

Here are organizational snapshots of the nine associations that made up the study group:

AARP

Headquarters: Washington, D.C.

Founded: 1958 (as the American Association of Retired Persons) The acronym AARP is the official name of the organization and is not an abbreviation for a longer title.

Nature: AARP 501(c)(4), individual membership
The AARP Foundation, 501(c)(3) organization
ASI, a wholly-owned taxable subsidiary

Scope: National

Members: 36 million

Chapters: 2,400

Employees: 2,218

Board: 21

Annual Budget: $1,038.5 billion (AARP, The AARP Foundation, and ASI combined)

CEO: William D. Novelli, chief executive officer

Web Site: www.aarp.org

Mission: "AARP is dedicated to enhancing quality of life for all as we age. We lead positive social change and deliver value to members through information, advocacy and service."

American College of Cardiology (ACC)

Headquarters: Washington, D.C.

Founded: 1949

Nature: 501(c)(3), professional

Scope: International

Members: 33,000

Chapters: 39

Employees: 260

Board: 600 (30-member Board of Trustees)

Annual Budget: $65 million

CEO: *vacant at the time of printing*

Web Site: www.acc.org

Mission: "The mission of the American College of Cardiology is to advocate for quality cardiovascular care—through education, research promotion, development and application of standards and guidelines—and to influence health care policy."

Core Values:

- *Professionalism:* The interests of patients are primary.
- *Knowledge:* The College must promote growth, dissemination, and application of knowledge about cardiovascular medicine.
- *Value of the cardiovascular specialist:* The cardiovascular profession makes a distinct contribution to medical care that should be recognized and enhanced.
- *Integrity:* Honesty, compliance with legal requirements, and ethical behavior are essential in all activities.
- *Member driven:* The College and its major activities must be led by active members and must promote volunteerism.
- *Inclusiveness:* The College involves a broad range of volunteers reflecting the composition of its membership.

American Dental Association (ADA)

Headquarters: Chicago, Illinois
Founded: 1859
Nature: 501(c)(6), professional
Scope: National
Members: 152,000
Chapters: 586
Employees: 428
Board: 22
Annual Budget: $102 million
CEO: James B. Bramson, executive director
Web Site: www.ada.org

Vision: "The American Dental Association: The oral health authority committed to the public and the profession."

Mission: "The ADA is the professional association of dentists committed to the public's oral health, ethics, science, and professional advancement; leading a unified profession through initiatives in advocacy, education, research, and the development of standards."

Associated General Contractors of America (AGC)

Headquarters: Arlington, Virginia

Founded: 1918

Nature: 501(c)(6), trade

Scope: National

Members: 33,000

Chapters: 98

Employees: 72

Board: 667 (24-member Executive Board)

Annual Budget: $417 million

CEO: Stephen E. Sandherr, chief executive officer

Web Site: www.agc.org

Mission: "The Associated General Contractors of America, the voice of the construction industry, is an organization of qualified construction contractors and industry-related companies dedicated to skill, integrity, and responsibility. Operating in partnership with its chapters, the association provides a full range of services satisfying the needs and concerns of its members, thereby improving the quality of construction and protecting the public interest."

Girl Scouts of the USA (GSUSA)

Headquarters: New York, New York
Founded: 1912
Nature: 501(c)(3), individual membership
Scope: National
Members: 3.6 million
Chapters: 310
Employees: 436
Board: 40 (10-member Executive Committee)
Annual Budget: $54.9 million operating budget (2006)
CEO: Kathy Cloninger, chief executive officer
Web Site: www.gsusa.org

Vision: "We are the experts on girls and their best advocates. We have what it takes to bring Girl Scouting to every girl. We are a forward-thinking and well-managed organization, taking the risks necessary to fulfill the Girl Scout Purpose. We are the first choice for girls and those who care about girls."

Purpose: "The purpose of Girl Scouts is inspiring girls with the highest ideals of character, conduct, patriotism, and service so that they may become happy and resourceful citizens."

Mission: "Girl Scouts of the USA is the world's pre-eminent organization dedicated solely to girls—all girls—where, in an accepting and nurturing environment, girls build character and skills for success in the real world. In partnership with committed adult volunteers, Girl Scouts cultivate their full individual potential. The qualities they develop in Girl Scouting—leadership, values, social conscience, and conviction about their own self-worth—serve them all their lives."

National Association of Counties (NACo)

Headquarters: Washington, D.C.

Founded: 1935

Nature: 501(c)(4), trade

Scope: National

Members: 2,185

Employees: 85

Board: 120 (5-member Executive Committee)

Annual Budget: $22 million

CEO: Larry E. Naake, executive director

Web Site: www.naco.org

Vision: "The NACo vision is to be an effective voice for America's counties in our nation's capital and to support counties and county officials in their efforts to provide improved programs and services to their residents."

Mission: "NACo is a full-service organization that provides an extensive line of services including legislative, research, and technical, as well as public affairs assistance to its members. The association acts as a liaison with other levels of government, works to improve public understanding of counties, serves as a national advocate for counties, and provides them with resources to help them find innovative methods to meet the challenges they face."

Ohio Society of Certified Public Accountants (OSCPA)

Headquarters: Dublin, Ohio

Founded: 1908

Nature: 501(c)(6), professional

Scope: State

Members: 23,000

Employees: 50

Board: 17

Annual Budget: $8 million

CEO: J. Clarke Price, CAE, president

Web Site: www.ohioscpa.com

Core Purpose: "CPAs…Making sense of a changing and complex world."

Vision: "CPAs are the trusted professionals who enable people and organizations to shape their future. Combining insight with integrity, CPAs deliver value by

- Communicating the total picture with clarity and objectivity
- Translating complex information into critical knowledge
- Anticipating and creating opportunities
- Designing pathways that transform vision into reality."

Radiological Society of North America (RSNA)

Headquarters: Oak Brook, Illinois
Founded: 1915
Nature: 501(c)(3), professional
Scope: International
Members: 38,000
Employees: 140
Board: 8
Annual Budget: $39.4 million
CEO: Dave Fellers, CAE, executive director
Web Site: www.rsna.org

Vision: "The RSNA aspires to be the premier professional association in radiology dedicated to science and education."

Mission: "The RSNA, an association of radiologists, radiation oncologists, and related scientists, is committed to excellence in patient care through education and research."

Core Values:
- Integrity
- Excellence
- Professionalism
- Leadership
- Innovation
- Service to the patient

Society for Human Resource Management (SHRM)

Headquarters: Alexandria, Virginia

Founded: 1948 (as the American Society for Personnel Administration)

Nature: 501(c)(6), professional

Scope: International

Members: 210,000

Chapters: 550

Employees: 300

Board: 11–15

Annual Budget: $95 million

CEO: Susan R. Meisinger, SPHR, president and chief executive officer

Web Site: www.shrm.org

Mission: "SHRM serves the needs of the human resource management professional by providing the most essential and comprehensive set of resources available. In addition, the Society is committed to advancing the human resource profession and the capabilities of all human resource professionals to ensure that HR is an essential and effective partner in developing and executing organizational strategy."

Financial Comparisons

The tables on the following pages offer a financial snapshot of all the organizations within the study and comparison groups. Please note that the data are all from 2002, the year for which the most complete data were available.

RATIO	❶ RESERVES: TOTAL EXPENSE	❷ NET REVENUE: TOTAL EXPENSE	❸ DUES REVENUE: TOTAL REVENUE	❹ DUES REVENUE: TOTAL MEMBERS	❺ TOTAL REVENUE: TOTAL STAFF	❻ TOTAL EXPENSE: TOTAL STAFF	❼ NON-DUES REVENUE: TOTAL STAFF
Study Group 1	80.42%	-3.06%	7.79%	129	245,108	252,836	226,007
Comparison Group 1	23.01%	3.55%	33.00%	110	163,702	158,088	109,680
Study Group 2	116.55%	-16.27%	18.52%	288	198,586	237,166	161,803
Comparison Group 2	79.12%	-2.74%	24.02%	286	173,597	178,482	131,901
Study Group 3	119.59%	-3.70%	70.92%	277	215,147	223,422	62,575
Comparison Group 3	29.71%	7.37%	72.77%	431	159,728	148,765	43,497
Study Group 4	68.48%	13.08%	23.33%	1,838	223,947	197,471	171,707
Comparison Group 4	-6.94%	-1.62%	8.97%	38,873	148,319	150,763	135,020
Study Group 5	24.33%	1.75%	51.40%	157	155,304	152,630	75,478
Comparison Group 5	177.27%	7.37%	79.86%	102	141,934	132,196	28,591
Study Group 6	108.50%	14.84%	37.60%	152	301,175	262,261	187,931
Comparison Group 6	4.79%	-0.46%	13.33%	473	255,796	256,508	221,754
Study Group 7	84.43%	0.87%	52.28%	432	206,042	202,693	98,318
Comparison Group 7	22.29%	-16.52%	15.75%	173	178,959	214,367	150,768
Study Group 8	155.23%	-13.36%	39.44%	7	134,840	155,634	81,654
Comparison Group 8	79.47%	-7.75%	0%	0	144,166	156,281	144,166
Study Group 9	53.51%	33.15%	36.00%	1	16,793	12,612	7,558
Comparison Group 9	21.51%	0.25%	0%	0	223,968	223,406	221,832

RATIO	RESERVES: TOTAL EXPENSE	NET REVENUE: TOTAL EXPENSE	DUES REVENUE: TOTAL REVENUE	DUES REVENUE: TOTAL MEMBERS	TOTAL REVENUE: TOTAL STAFF	TOTAL EXPENSE: TOTAL STAFF	NON-DUES REVENUE: TOTAL STAFF
Average Study	90.12%	3.03%	37.48%	365	188,549	188,525	119,226
Average Comparison	47.80%	-1.17%	27.52%	4,494	176,685	179,873	131,912
Median Study	84.43%	0.87%	37.60%	157	206,042	202,693	98,318
Median Comparison	23.01%	-0.46%	15.75%	173	163,702	158,088	135,020

Notes on Data Columns

❶ Reserves = Unrestricted Net Assets (Balance Sheet)
   Total Expense = Total Expenses (Statement of Activities)

❷ Net Revenue = Total Revenue less Total Expense less Unrealized Gains / (or plus Losses) on Investments (Statement of Activities)
   Total Expense = Total Expenses (Statement of Activities)

❸ Dues Revenue = Total Revenue from all membership dues categories (Statement of Activities)
   Total Revenue = Total Revenue less Unrealized Gains / (or plus Losses) on Investments (Statement of Activities)

❹ Dues Revenue = Total Revenue from all membership dues categories (Statement of Activities)
   Members = Total dues paying members (or total members if that is all that is available) (Other Data)

❺ Total Revenue = Total Revenue less Unrealized Gains / (or plus Losses) on Investments (Statement of Activities)
   Total Staff = Full Time Equivalents (Other Data)

❻ Total Expense = Total Expenses (Statement of Activities)
   Total Staff = Full Time Equivalents (Other Data)

❼ Non-Dues Revenue = Total Revenue (see above) - Dues Revenue (see above)
   Total Staff = Full Time Equivalents (Other Data)

Average Number of Years in the Red vs. Years in the Black: Study vs. Comparison Groups

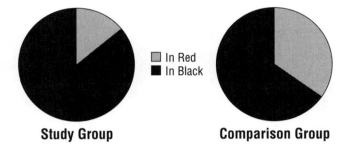

□ In Red
■ In Black

Study Group   **Comparison Group**

Research Timeline and Tools

Research Timeline

February 2002   Jim Collins, coauthor of *Built to Last* and author of *Good to Great,* speaks at DigitalNow conference.

August 2002   Members of Research Committee of The Center for Association Leadership (then the ASAE Foundation) meet with Collins to discuss possibility of applying his research methodology to a multiyear research project involving associations. Collins agrees to provide guidance and serve as mentor during the project.

November 2002   Research Committee submits proposal to the board of The Center for Association Leadership (then the ASAE Foundation) requesting funding for the Measures of Success project.

January 2003   After receiving approval to pursue the project, Research Committee forms Measures of Success Task Force and names Michael E. Gallery, Ph.D., CAE, as chairman.

February–June 2003   Random (nth name) sample of 1,000 members of ASAE (CEOs, number-two executives, and industry leaders) invited to participate in the jurying process. They receive a request to nominate five associations that are viewed as "benchmark" organizations, have persisted against difficult circumstances, and enjoy active and engaged members. Survey garners 324 responses—a 32 percent response rate at the 95 percent confidence level—and generates list of 506 associations. A natural break in the rankings produces a list of 104 top vote-getters.

August 2003   Collins meets with task force to provide guidance on selection criteria for study and comparison associations.

September 2003 Two recent college graduates hired as research investigators to work full time on the project.

October 2003   Letters sent to top 105 associations identified through the jurying process, inviting them to participate and requesting preliminary membership and financial data.

November 2003   Follow-up letters sent to associations that had not yet responded.

December 2003   Overall, 55 associations respond (53 percent response rate), with 47 indicating a willingness to participate and 8 opting to withdraw from consideration. Three other associations are eliminated because of tax status, age (less than 20 years old), and status as an allied society.

January 2004   From the remaining pool of 36 associations, the task force selects 22 as meeting its criteria for financial and membership health (more years in the black than in the red and growth or consistent maintenance of membership/market share numbers). The other 14 associations are excused from the study.

February 2004   Task force members personally contact the CEOs of seven associations that did not respond to the invitation to participate. Research investigators begin collecting 15 years of financial and membership data for associations that have agreed to participate and signed the Institutional Agreement.

March 2004	Task force members define 11 areas to be studied for each association and develop a series of questions to be asked during on-site visits by research investigators. They also develop nine research pairings, matching each association in the study group with one in the comparison group. To keep focus on aggregate results rather than one-on-one pairings, task force decides not to publicly acknowledge which associations form the comparison group.
May 2004	Research instruments and interview questions to guide data collection in the 11 areas are developed.
July–September 2004	Research team field tests and finalizes research instruments and interview questions at four beta-tested associations.
October 2004	Research investigators begin site visits to associations in both the study and comparison groups.
December 2004	Task force meets with Collins, who reviews his research methodology and outlines a process for analyzing the data.
March–May 2005	With majority of site visits and interviews completed, research investigators begin compiling detailed reports and analyses of data.
June–August 2005	Two task force members assigned to each research pairing; these teams review researchers' reports and interview transcripts as well as materials submitted by participating associations.
September 2005	Task force meets with Collins to share preliminary results of data analysis, identify gaps in information, and finalize remaining steps.
October–November 2005	Task force members conduct on-site visits to associations in both the study and comparison groups and interview CEOs to answer follow-up questions.

Research investigators complete data collection and analysis.

December 2005   Based on research reports, interviews, on-site visits, and the materials review, each team member compiles an individual dossier on one pairing of study and comparison organizations.

January 2006   Drawing on their individual dossiers, members of each team compile a team dossier to share with other task force members. Measures of Success Task Force conducts final meeting to analyze results of matched pairings and generate conclusions.

Complete List of Documents Requested

DOCUMENT	DESCRIPTION
ABOUT THE VISION	
Vision statement	Statement of vision for the organization
Value statement	Statement of value for the organization
Mission statement	Statement of mission for the organization
Purpose statement	Statement of purpose for the organization
Goal statements	Statement of goals for the organization
Transcripts of speeches	Transcribed speeches from CEO/ED or President/President-Elect
Transcripts of public addresses	Transcribed speeches from CEO/ED or President/President-Elect
MARKETS, COMPETITORS, AND THE ENVIRONMENT	
Staff allocated to market research	Number of staff assigned to market research
Budget allocated to market research	Budget dollars assigned to market research
Industry studies	Studies, reports on the industry conducted by the organization
Market research utilization	Internal documents regarding how industry-related research is used
Membership studies	Studies, reports on the membership/donors conducted by the organization
Membership surveys	Surveys conducted specifically within the membership
Membership research	Internal research done on the membership or member metrics
Membership research utilization	Internal documents regarding how member-ship related research is used
Member dues	Member dues from 1988–2003

Records of mergers within membership	Documentation of mergers effecting the membership
Recruitment efforts	Recruitment and retention plans, programs used to recruit members
Membership services to nonmembers	What services are offered to nonmembers? Is there a difference in how the service is offered?
Environmental scans	Environmental scans conducted on factors effecting the organization
Benchmarking data	Benchmarking data, metrics used by the organization
Questionnaires and surveys	Any questionnaires or surveys used by the organization to assess the membership, staff
Circulation of magazine	Circulation of the magazine from 1988–2003
Core competencies for members	Defined core competencies for membership if applicable
Member satisfaction studies	Studies pertaining to member satisfaction
Member demographics	Demographics of membership
Staff allocated to marketing	Number of staff assigned to marketing
Budget allocated to marketing	Budget dollars assigned to marketing
Marketing plans	Internal marketing plans used by the organization
Member/donor retention goals	Measurable goals for member/donor retention
Member/donor retention performance	Realistic performance as compared to goals for member/donor retention
Member/donor acquisition goals	Measurable goals for total member/donor growth
Member/donor acquisition performance	Realistic performance as compared to goals for member/donor growth

Enrollment numbers	Total membership 1988–2003
Membership numbers	Broken down membership number by category 1988–2003
Long-term marketing plans	Internal longer-term marketing plans used by the organization
Marketing initiatives	Programs used for marketing to members
Marketing strategies	Strategies, planning for marketing to members
Marketing implementation	Internal documents regarding how members were marketed to
Media kits	Media kits for Annual Meetings, magazine, journal advertising

ORGANIZATIONAL ARRANGEMENTS

Organization chart that includes board, staff, and volunteers	Graphic representation of volunteer-to-staff relationship
Bylaws and historical amendments	Organization bylaws and amendments made 1988–2003
Articles of incorporation	Articles of incorporation for the organization
List of outsourced functions	List of functions outsourced by the organization
List of consultants used	List of consultants the organization has used
Job descriptions for all jobs	Description of staff positions in the organization
List of national officers	List of board members in the organization from 1988–2003
List of national staff	List of employees 1988–2003

USE OF TECHNOLOGY

Staff allocated to technology (qualifications and salary)	Number of staff assigned to technology functions of the organization
Budget allocated to technology	Budget dollars assigned to technology

Annual expenditures on hardware	Expenditures on hardware 1988–2003
Annual expenditures on software	Expenditures on software 1988–2003
Annual expenditures on tech support	Expenditures on tech support 1988–2003
All technologies used	List of technologies used internally
Major technological advances	Highlighted major technology advances for the organization 1988–2003
BUSINESS STRATEGY/STRATEGIC PROCESS	
Published info on strategic plans	Strategic Plans, operational plans
Published info on strategic planning process	Internal documentation on planning process
Internal meeting minutes	Internal staff meeting minutes
Crisis management documents	Planning, documentation of Crisis Management policies
Strategic partnerships	List of strategic partnerships
PRODUCTS AND SERVICES	
Major vendor services	List of major vendors used by the organization
Annual conference revenue	Annual conference revenue 1988–2003
Annual conference expenses	Annual conference expenses 1988–2003
Member awards programs	List of award programs for members
Magazine distribution	Distribution of magazine 1988–2003
Journal distribution	Distribution of journals 1988–2003
Certification materials	Materials pertaining to certifications awarded by the organization

Program design	Documents on new program design, how programs go from conceptualization to implementation
Program development	Documents discussing how programs are developed and implemented
List of products and services	List of products and services offered by organization
Sales history	Revenue generated from sales of goods 1988–2003
Market research for products	Documents pertaining to market research on specific products
Process for identifying new products and services	Documents on the process for bringing new programs forward
Annual meeting schedules	Annual meeting schedules, how the time is used at an annual meeting
LEADERSHIP	
List of Board members, terms, and roles	List of Board members 1988–2003, term definitions and responsibilities of Board members
Policies and procedures for Board	Policies and procedures manuals for the Board
List of standing committees and members	List of committees for the organization and members of those committees, including purpose
List of ad hoc committees and members	List of ad hoc committees, task forces and members of those committees, including purpose
Board evaluations	Evaluation documents for the Board
Role of staff in Board work	Documentation of role staff plays in Board meetings, implementing Board decisions
Board meeting minutes	Meeting minutes from Board meetings 1988–2003
CEO contract	Contract of the current CEO
Board of Directors bylaws	Bylaws for the Board and changes 1988–2003

Recognition and acknowledgement of volunteers	Documents pertaining to Awards and recognition for volunteer leaders
Board of Directors self-assessment	Self-assessment documents for Board
Documents from Board orientation program	Board orientation materials

<table>
<tr><td colspan="2">COMMUNITY AND CULTURE</td></tr>
<tr><td>Demographic data of staff</td><td>Listing of staff by tenure, age, race, gender, education, title, and grade</td></tr>
<tr><td>Number of staff yearly</td><td>Number of staff 1988–2003</td></tr>
<tr><td>Policies and procedures manual</td><td>Staff policies and procedures manuals 1988–2003</td></tr>
<tr><td>History of lawsuits</td><td>Documentation of recorded lawsuits for the organization</td></tr>
<tr><td>Succession planning process</td><td>Defined succession planning documents</td></tr>
<tr><td>List of training events and programs</td><td>List of internal training events and programs for staff</td></tr>
<tr><td>History of staff restructuring and layoffs</td><td>Documentation of internal staff restructuring and layoffs</td></tr>
<tr><td>Performance appraisals for staff</td><td>Performance appraisal documents for staff—blank or without names</td></tr>
<tr><td>Benefits plans for staff</td><td>Staff benefits</td></tr>
<tr><td>Exit reviews</td><td>Employee exit reviews—blank or without names</td></tr>
<tr><td>Internal awards, criteria, and winners</td><td>Documents pertaining to staff awards given and winners</td></tr>
<tr><td>External awards, criteria, and winners</td><td>Documents pertaining to member awards programs</td></tr>
<tr><td>Culture statements</td><td>Statement of the culture for the organization</td></tr>
<tr><td>Code of Ethics</td><td>Code of Ethics for the organization and changes 1988–2003</td></tr>
</table>

Code of ethics enforcement	Documentation for enforcement of Code of Ethics
Diversity programs/initiatives	Documentation/materials regarding diversity programs and initiatives for the organization

FINANCIAL INFORMATION

Statement of Financial Position	Statement of Financial Position 1988–2003
Balance Sheets	Balance Sheets 1988–2003
Statement of Cash Flows	Statement of Cash Flows 1988–2003
Budgets	Budgets 1988–2003
Form 990	Form 990s 1988–2003
Annual Reports	Annual Reports 1988–2003
Source of nondues revenue	Sources of nondues revenue 1988–2003
Donations and grants	Documentation of donations and grants for the organization
Investment policies	Documented Investment policies for the organization
Fundraising initiatives	Documents outlining fundraising initiatives for the organization
Liability insurance	Documented Liability policies for the organization
Request for exemption	Request for exemption form
Reserve policy	Documented Reserve policies for the organization
Financial audits	External audits of financial disclosures 1988–2003

PUBLIC POLICY

Amicus Curiae briefs	Amicus Curiae briefs presented by the organization
PAC bylaws	Bylaws of the PAC if applicable
Financial disclosures on PAC if applicable	PAC treasurer notes, receipts, and expenditures

Other PAC information	Other documents related to funding of PAC, committee meeting minutes

OTHER DOCUMENTS COLLECTED	
Chapter numbers	Number of chapters 1988–2003
Member benefits	What are the benefits of membership?
Awards received by organization	Any documentation of awards received by the organization
Membership application	New member applications, What does a prospective member receive?
Constitution	Constitution for the organization if applicable
List of Executive Committee members	List of Executive Committee members 1988–2003
Policy Statements	Policy/position statements made by the organizations

On-Site Interview Questions

The following structured set of interview questions was developed to ensure consistency. The research investigators spoke with the CEO and other senior and support staff representing a range of tenure at the association. These interviews were transcribed and attached to the detailed report prepared for each of the 18 associations.

Vision, Mission, and Purpose

How would you characterize the basic reason for this organization's existence? Has it changed over time?

Describe a difficult choice or important decision you have had to make. Did the vision, values, mission, or goals come into play in your decision or choice?

Markets, Competitors, and the Environment

Tell me about your markets (members and suppliers). Has the composition of either group changed over time? How has your organization adjusted to these changes?

How do your members and suppliers contribute to the success of your organization?

Who are your chief competitors? What do you view as their main competitive strengths and weaknesses, compared to this organization?

Do you perform formal scanning or market research? If you do conduct research, can you give me an example of how it was used?

Organizing Arrangements

Describe the relationship between the board, the CEO, and the staff. Has the structure, size, or style of governance changed since you came into this organization in your current capacity? Are there any new types of structures?

Have staffing levels and/or structure changed over the past 15 years?

How are board members and officers chosen? How is the CEO chosen?

Use of Technology

What have been the most important technological "events" to affect your organization during the past 15 years?

What has been your association's traditional approach to technology expenditures? Describe any major technology initiatives since you've been here.

Of which technologies does your organization make the greatest use?

Describe your organization's attitude toward technology: "early adopter," "early majority," "late majority," or "laggard"? Your members' attitude?

Business Strategy/Strategic Process

Over the past 15 years, can you describe two instances where the organization was forced by external events to cope with major change?

How did you define success? By that definition, was the change successful? Did you conduct any formal evaluation or measurement to assess the results?

Can you describe two examples where the organization initiated such change on its own? If so, why did you decide to undertake the change? How did you define success? By that definition, was the change successful? Did you conduct any formal evaluation or measurement to assess the results?

Looking back, is there anything that you wish you, or your organization, had done differently? Is there anything you are particularly proud of?

Products and Services

Describe the organization's "signature" products or services. Can you explain the development process and who was involved?

What, if any, role do members have in the product development process? What about board, staff, and suppliers?

Have you had any product failures? If so, what did you learn from the experience?

Have you engaged in any joint ventures or strategic alliances with other groups? If so, what prompted your decision to do so? What has worked well, and what hasn't?

Leadership

For the CEO:

What characteristics would you use to describe yourself and your leadership style? What do you consider to be your strengths and weaknesses?

Could you describe the process by which you were selected to lead this organization? Who made the ultimate decision, and who participated? What was it like—that is, how was it the same as previous experiences, and how was it different?

How do people move up in this organization? Is there a formal succession plan?

For Other Staff:

Which among the current CEO's qualities, skills, or experience were most appealing to the selection team? What were your feelings on this decision?

In terms of the leadership model/style here, what do you like and what do you dislike?

How do people move up in this organization? Is there a formal succession plan?

How would you describe the relationship between your CEO or leaders and the board? What works well? What doesn't? Why?

Culture and Community

What advice would you give to a new employee or volunteer entering this organization about how to be successful?

Thinking about your job, what are you most excited about? Most worried about? Why?

Based on what you have told them, how do you imagine your friends or family would describe this association as an employer?

How much contact do you have with members on a daily basis? What is the nature and tone of the interaction?

Financial Issues

Over the past 15 years, how has your organization's financial situation changed? What internal or external forces influenced these changes?

What event in the past 15 years has impacted your financial direction? Was this event anticipated or was it a shock? How long were its effects felt? Were there any countermeasures taken as a result? What was learned from this experience?

How do you determine capital and operational expenditures?

Explain the involvement of staff and volunteers in the financial management process.

How do you evaluate and report the impact of economic and budget factors on financial planning, investment policies, and financial performance?

How do you set and manage your reserve policy?

Physical Setting and Location

How and when was your association's main office selected and by whom?

Is either setting or location of your organization's main office important to its mission?

Does the internal layout reflect any particular value or philosophy held by your association? Does it contradict any value or philosophy?

Public Policy

When an issue impacts your membership, what actions are taken and how quickly? Who makes the decisions to move forward with major decisions?

How involved are members in your PAC? How are contributions primarily allocated?

How does your membership support the public policy initiatives of the organization? Do the members make an impact on public policy initiatives?

Who identifies the public policy initiatives of the organization? How do you determine the need for grassroots activities? How are they implemented and evaluated?

Follow-up Interview Questions for CEOs

A follow-up, on-site visit was conducted to gather more information, including getting a better feel for each organization's environment, such as culture and physical setting. This visit included an interview with each organization's CEO. The following structured set of interview questions was developed to ensure consistency.

1. Please describe the relationship between strategic planning and budgeting in your association.
   - How involved are your members in driving change?
   - How are priorities set? Do you believe that priorities change as elected leaders change?
   - How is the strategic plan communicated throughout the organization to ensure its implementation?
   - How do you integrate the strategic plan into day-to-day operations?
   - How do you evaluate the outcomes of the strategic plan?
   - Has your planning/budgeting process changed within the last 5 to 10 years? If so, how?

2. What steps do you take to ensure you have the right people on your staff to carry out the strategic plan?

3. Please provide two or three examples of how implementation of the strategic plan has led to change in your organization.

4. Looking back over the last 10 years, what factors have contributed to your organization's success? What factors have impeded its success?

5. When you became the CEO, what were the top 3 changes you wanted to make? Why? What level of success did you achieve with those changes?

6. How does the board evaluate your success as the CEO?

7. Explain the process your association uses to identify, pursue, and finalize strategic alliances and other partnerships.

8. How does your association create and nurture future leaders within the membership?

9. At the end of the day, how do you measure the success of your organization?

Individual Dossier

After completing the supplemental data collection, each task force team compiled a dossier that analyzed the similarities and differences between one matched pair (one study association and one comparison association). The entire task force reviewed all the dossiers as a starting point for generating findings.

Study Organization: _____

Comparison Organization: _____

1. What are the obvious differences between the two organizations?

2. What are the similarities between the two organizations?

3. In both organizations, what developments, occurrences, activities, etc., call into question the prevailing "conventional wisdom" within the association management field?

4. Share the details of at least one success story from the study group; if possible, contrast it with a similar situation at the comparison group that did not have as positive an outcome.

5. What is the essence of this particular pairing? In other words, "Why is one gold and the other silver or bronze?"

Frequently Asked Questions

1. What relevance does Jim Collins' research, conducted in the for-profit sector, have to voluntary associations?

Although many have studied the sources of excellence in for-profit organizations, few have addressed the definition—let alone the sources—of success in voluntary membership associations. A number of reasons for this informational deficit come to mind.

First, publicly traded companies are legally required to submit detailed financial reports to the Securities & Exchange Commission (SEC) on a quarterly basis. Additionally, the stock market (stock price) and the marketplace (sales volume, gross and net income, sources of revenue, and so forth) provide standardized measures of corporate performance. Because the SEC has standardized reporting requirements in terms of scope, content, types of information, unit of analysis (by corporation, by division, by geography), you can make apples-to-apples comparisons among various companies.

In contrast, most associations have a combination of 501(c)(6), 501(c)(3), and privately held, for-profit divisions housed under one umbrella. Requirements for reporting to the government are typically less frequent and less detailed. The true financial status of an association may also be more difficult to discern, since the umbrella organization may be composed of several smaller ones, each with a different legal structure and tax status. The diverse legal structures and inconsistent reporting requirements make it much more difficult to objectively assess or compare different associations' performance.

While solvency ensures an association's survival, making a profit is not its primary reason for existence. By their very nature, associations are mission-driven organizations whose fundamental *raisons d'être* are conceptual and intangible and thus, difficult to quantify. Even if their tax status didn't prohibit associations from explicit pursuit of profits, their own goals would.

Finally, rigorous, quantifiable research is expensive to conduct. Whereas for-profit businesses have comparatively large research budgets, associations have less money to spend on this sort of activity.

2. How was the research team of association executives selected?

The research team was selected based on their experience, plus the scope, size, and type of their employing organization. Having a broad cross section of association executives and strategists was important to help us stay unbiased and objective. Because the study included varying types of organizations, we sought varying expertise to help us to understand and analyze the data from different perspectives.

3. What were your initial selection criteria for the associations in the study group?

Candidates for the study group need to have:

- Been in operation for at least 20 years;
- Finished more years in the black than in the red;
- Exhibited the ability to retain members, donors, or market share during the study period; and
- Had more than one CEO during the study period.

4. Why didn't you consider organizations that had one CEO for more than 15 years?

We attempted to follow as closely as possible the methodology Collins and Porras used in *Built to Last*. Like them, we were interested in identifying what factors contributed to an organization's greatness. We were looking for factors that were a part of the organization's fundamental structure and not a function of a specific product, service, or person.

For this reason, Collins and Porras selected to study companies founded before 1950. They argued that this time period would be sufficient to ensure a variety of products, services, and CEOs. Given the average age of associations as well as the length of time that associations maintain records, we believed that a 15-year period would better serve our needs.

5. How did you accommodate inconsistencies in reporting and collecting data from the associations over 15 years?

The quality and quantity of the information submitted varied across organizations. Because of the time period, some associations didn't have electronic records of materials, document retention policy did not require it to save the information, or documentation was simply insufficient to correlate with its counterpart.

Some organizations, such as AARP, Girl Scouts of the USA, and the Society for Human Resource Management, provided more information than we could possibly analyze in a couple of sittings. In an isolated case, an organization provided very minimal information. Our research investigators put their curiosity to work and searched for information through secondary sources. We attempted to locate the exact same information about each organization. In some cases, that simply wasn't possible.

No organization provided the entire 15 years of information exactly as requested. We are confident that the information received supports the concepts in this publication.

6. Why are there so few trade associations in the study?

We made every attempt to ensure that we had sufficient representation from trade, professional, and philanthropic organizations. Collins' work involved publicly traded companies. He had access to an abundance of public documents published by those companies as well as a massive amount of literature published in the popular press about his subjects.

We, on the other hand, were dealing with associations. The information we needed to review was not in the public domain. Our only means of acquiring it was through the voluntary cooperation of the associations. We identified several potential trade associations; however, we succeeded in gaining the cooperation of a few. Given that concern, we asked several representatives of trade associations to review our findings.

7. What was the stock price equivalent for associations?

Collins used stock price only in *Good to Great*. In *Built to Last*, Collins and Porras used a jurying process to identify great companies. Among the list generated from this process, they selected those companies that had been founded before 1950.

In *Good to Great*, Collins was interested in studying companies that had started out good and become great. What, he wondered, had they done differently than those companies who remained good?

Unlike his first study in which he used a jurying process to identify highly visionary companies, he realized that this study required the use of objective measures. He and his research team analyzed the stock performance of Fortune 500 companies. Among those, he identified 11 companies that realized and maintained a dramatic increase in their stock price while other companies in their industry maintained a good increase in their stock prices.

Our study employed the *Built to Last* methodology. Like Collins and Porras, we used a jurying process to identify an initial list of candidate organizations. From that list we selected remarkable organizations on the basis of three criteria:

- Financial performance as evidenced by consistently ending the year in the black

- Consistent member (or donor growth) and low member attrition
- Have existed for at least 15 years and had more than one CEO

8. How did you identify the conventional wisdoms?

Conventional wisdoms were identified based on the common themes and issues that arose during the review process. The conventional wisdoms were further vetted at a research retreat where we had an opportunity to write all the qualitative and quantitative information in aggregate to dispel myths that did not hold up against our research findings.

During one of its many meetings, members of the Measures of Success Task Force, all seasoned association executives and strategists, generated the following list of statements of conventional wisdom:

- One person should be at the top.
- Keep 50 percent of annual expenses in reserves.
- CEO should be an association professional.
- CEO should come from outside the organization rather than within.
- Don't get too far ahead of the membership.
- Elections should reflect the democratic process.
- Elected leaders should move through the ranks.
- Small boards are better than big boards.
- Organizations should be more member-driven than staff-driven.
- Be innovative/on the cutting edge.
- Run the association like a corporation.
- Engage in consensus decision making.
- Participatory management is best.
- CEO should take a back seat to the elected leader.
- CEO is always right.
- Have a one-year term for elected leaders.
- Association activities require constituent buy-in.

- Radical times require radical change.
- Proactive change is better than reactive change.
- The board sets the policy; the staff implements it.
- Staff should not be involved in selection of leaders.
- CEO has no vote on the board.
- Have a strategic plan.
- A higher market share is better.

During its final meeting, the task force compared its findings with this list to determine which statements, if any, were not consistent with those findings. The results of that analysis appear in Chapter 6— Old Saws and Fresh Cuts.

APPENDIX E

How to Measure the Measures

How well does your association perform on the seven measures?

This is an easy question to ask but a hard one to answer.

For example:

- Many of the qualities that exemplify remarkable associations are intangible. A "customer service culture" cannot be accurately measured by counting the number of "We love our members" plaques on the wall. Anyone can put up a plaque. Member focus is both an attitude and a set of practices.

- Several of the measures are not mutually exclusive. The presence of "dialogue and engagement" and the model of the "CEO as broker of ideas" both reflect an organizational culture that values candor, where people from all quarters may speak freely without fear of retribution and innovate without being seen as disrespecting authority.

- Several measures are innately subjective and inevitably influenced by one's role in the association. As an example, an association's product development team may perceive its efforts as being closely aligned with the mission, while those engaged in product marketing may see things quite differently.

Fortunately, none of these issues presents an insurmountable obstacle to an association willing to embark on an objective measurement program. Doing so first requires a commitment to:

- Invest the time, money, and effort required to do measurement properly.

- Communicate the results broadly and with candor.

- Foster change in the areas identified as problematic by the research. Asking for feedback and then ignoring or discounting the messages received can diminish your organization's credibility as well as its ability to gather honest feedback in the future.

Outlined below are several methods that can be used to ascertain how well an association is performing on each of the commitments and the criteria (measures) on which they are built. Some options are more ambitious and others are smaller, less expensive methods for conducting measurements.

Commitment to Purpose

Measure 1: A Customer Service Culture

Both organizational policies and processes and unrehearsed interactions with individual members consistently express a "We're here to serve you" attitude.

Potential Measurement Methods

- Develop a program to measure and analyze compliments and complaints. This is a simple and relatively inexpensive method of finding out what makes members feel valued and what engenders dissatisfaction.

- Administer the State of Community Assessment (SOCA) developed by ASAE & The Center for Association Leadership. Designed by and for associations, the assessment contains a wealth of information addressing this issue and numerous others featured in the seven measures.

- Conduct focus groups, using an independent moderator, with front-line employees at your association. Include those who answer the phones, who interact with members and/or volunteers at meetings, and so forth. Often, the people on the front lines know a great deal about members and the association's attitudes toward them. Typically, front-line employees are also willing to speak with candor.

Measure 2:
Alignment of Products and Services with Mission

The association's mission remains consistent, and the association's portfolio of products and services is consistent with its stated mission.

Potential Measurement Methods

- Identify the presence or absence of a written mission statement. Is there any evidence to suggest that the mission has played a meaningful role in shaping actions across time? Review minutes of meetings leading to and/or announcements of significant changes to see whether specific elements of the mission are mentioned.

- Look at major sources of income and areas of investment across a 10-year period. Do products and services that explicitly reflect the mission provide a major source of income? Has the association consistently invested time, money, and effort in the development of mission-consistent products and services?

- Conduct focus groups, using an independent moderator, organized around the topic: "What is our mission?" Hold focus groups with members, staff at all levels, and volunteers but do not tell them in advance that you will be asking this question.

Commitment to Analysis and Feedback

Measure 3: Data-Driven Strategies

Remarkable associations have developed an expertise in gathering information as well as processes for sharing and analyzing the data to deduce what actions the data point to taking.

Potential Measurement Methods

- Count the number of channels through which you gather information, the types of information collected, and the places in your organization that engage in such activities. You may use informal channels, such as conversations with members or colleagues, and/or formal market research studies. You may seek both qualitative data (from focus groups, for example) and structured, quantitative data in the form of surveys; the data may be collected at numerous points throughout your organization, including human resources, member relations, customer service, and so forth. The more you find in each area, the better.

- Determine what happens to the information collected through the various methods. Does it ever move beyond the point of contact? To begin to tap its promise, information must be recorded, shared, and analyzed in relation to information from other sources.

- Next, ask, "Does the information get communicated? If so, how is it communicated and to whom?" Information can be a powerful tool for framing and motivating action. Far from hurting your organization, transparency engenders trust, motivates change, and fosters innovation.

- Exercise discipline to collect accurate data. Specifically, record the information you collect in a standardized format and adhere to professional standards when conducting formal market research. Designing and administering a survey correctly requires skill and formal training; this responsibility should not be assigned to people who are not fully qualified. Remarkable associations believe in good, solid research and commit the resources necessary to do it well.

Measure 4: Dialogue and Engagement

An internal conversation continually occurs among staff and volunteers about the organization's direction and priorities.

Potential Measurement Methods

- Conduct an employee survey, using either a standardized or customized survey program, to learn about the state of communication in your association. Ideally, seek the advice of an independent expert who has advanced training in psychometrics and the particular quirks of employee survey management. (Hint: confidentiality issues loom large in employee surveys). This expert should not have any institutional ties that could bias his or her advice, such as being employed by a company that sells survey instruments.

- Use "360° assessments" of randomly selected employees, volunteers, staff, members, and suppliers as another means of discerning the state of communication in your association. Again, many such instruments are available; ideally, seek the advice of an independent expert before making your selection.

Measure 5: CEO as Broker of Ideas

Although the CEO may be visionary, what's more important is that the CEO facilitates visionary thinking throughout the organization.

Potential Measurement Methods

- Review the tenure of current and past CEOs: Can you find examples of ideas, new products or services, or initiatives that were generated by someone else? If so, how many were there? Did any of these initiatives receive institutional support in the form of time, money, and/or publicity? If so, how did the level of support compare to initiatives that originated with the CEO? How many of these proposals were ultimately implemented?

- On a daily, weekly, or monthly basis, determine how much time the CEO spends, outside his or her office and/or the association's headquarters, listening to and interacting with various stakeholders. How much time does the CEO spend learning about the world beyond the borders of the association? How often does he or she present truly new material, in any forum, for review and discussion? A simple count of such events can be highly instructive.

Commitment to Action

Measure 6: Organizational Adaptability

Great associations learn from and respond to change; although willing to change, they also know what not to change.

Potential Measurement Methods
Answering these questions can help assess the association's level of adaptability during times of change.

1. How does the association monitor and respond to future trends, threats, and opportunities likely to impact the association environment?

2. How open have the association's leaders been in discussing changes affecting the organization's environment?

3. In addressing the changes, did the association leaders seek input from staff/employees, members, volunteers, and/or the board? If so, from whom?

4. Has the association faced a financial dilemma, a sudden and dramatic loss in membership, or a public relations issue? If so,

what, if any, were the lessons learned and how has it affected the organization's strategic decisions?

According to research by C.R. Wanberg and J.T. Banas reported in the *Journal of Applied Psychology* ("Predictors and Outcomes of Openness to Changes in a Reorganizing Workplace," February 2000), resilient organizations do the following in times of crisis:

- Acknowledge that positive and negative changes exist, while projecting realistic optimism.
- Provide information generously, to all concerned.
- Invite participation on the part of all stakeholders in learning from and adapting to change, while simultaneously lending social and personal support to all affected.

Thus, answers to the first set of questions are proxy measures for adaptability and should be posed to all stakeholders.

Measure 7: Alliance Building

Associations that are secure and confident in their own right seek partners and projects that complement their mission and purpose.

Potential Measurement Methods

Measuring your association's ability to build successful alliances goes beyond basic counting. For instance:

1. How many alliances has the association sought during the past five years and why?

2. How many alliances have been formalized during that same time?

3. Who are the association's unconventional partners?

4. When seeking alliances, does the organization have a list of criteria describing the type of alliance it wishes to form and the nature

of its relationship to the association's strengths, weaknesses, mission, vision, and/or goals?

5. With any alliance ultimately formed, did the association establish metrics for success in advance?

6. Has the association ever evaluated an alliance partner and ultimately decided to decline? Why?

The answers to these questions will help an association begin to assess the extent to which any alliances were considered in terms of their alignment with mission and goals, core competencies, and the association's willingness to invest in careful planning to enhance success.

Sir Francis Bacon noted that knowledge is power. Like any other powerful tool, the information embodied by the seven measures confers power on the user *only* if collected carefully and ethically and used responsibly—in the service of the association's stakeholders and its goals.

Participating Organizations

ASAE & The Center for Association Leadership gratefully acknowledge the following organizations for generously sharing data and information for consideration in this research study:

AARP

The Aluminum Association

American Academy of Family Physicians

American Automobile Association

American College of Cardiology

American College of Healthcare Executives

American College of Surgeons

American Dental Association

American Diabetes Association

American Petroleum Institute

American Psychological Association

American Society of Civil Engineers

American Speech-Language-Hearing Association

American Thyroid Association

American Veterinary Medical Association

Associated Builders and Contractors

Associated General Contractors of America

Association of Healthcare Philanthropy

Boys and Girls Club of America

California Association of Realtors

Conference of State Bank Supervisors

Council of Christian Colleges and Universities

Edison Electric Institute

Equipment Leasing Association

Florida Chamber of Commerce

Girl Scouts of the USA

Illinois Association of Realtors

International City/County Management Association

Meeting Professionals International

Michigan Association of Home Builders

National 4-H Council

National American Indian Housing Council

National Association of Chain Drug Stores

National Association of College Stores

National Association of Counties

National Association of Secondary School Principals

National Association of Social Workers

National Association of Wheat Growers

National Business Travel Association

National Collegiate Athletic Association

National Paint and Coating Association

National Restaurant Association

National Roofing Contractors Association

National School Boards Association

Ohio Society of Certified Public Accountants

Radiological Society of North America

Save the Children

Society for Human Resource Management

Southern Association of Orthodontists

Southland Regional Association of Realtors

United Way

Donor Acknowledgments

Thanks to generous donations from associations and industry partners, ASAE & The Center for Association Leadership is able to conduct its strategic research agenda. Together, our members and industry partners are building a better tomorrow.

LEAD SPONSORS AND FOUNDING PARTNERS

Marriott International	www.marriott.com
J. Willard & Alice S. Marriott Foundation	www.marriott.com
Starwood Hotels & Resorts Worldwide	www.starwoodhotels.com

FOUNDING PARTNERS—CONVENTION AND VISITOR BUREAUS

Anaheim/Orange County Visitors & Convention Bureau	www.anaheimoc.org
Atlanta Convention & Visitors Bureau	www.atlanta.net
Atlantic City Convention & Visitors Authority	www.atlanticcitynj.com
Greater Boston Convention & Visitors Bureau, Inc.	www.bostonusa.com
Chicago Convention & Tourism Bureau	www.meetinchicago.com
Hawaii Visitors & Convention Bureau	www.gohawaii.com
Greater Miami Convention & Visitors Bureau	www.gmcvb.com
LA INC The Convention & Visitors Bureau	www.lacvb.com
Las Vegas Convention & Visitors Authority	www.lvcva.com
Nashville Convention & Visitors Bureau	www.nashville.com
NYC and Company	www.nycvisit.com
San Diego Convention and Visitors Bureau	www.sandiego.com
Seattle's Convention and Visitors Bureau	www.seeseattle.org
St. Louis Convention and Visitors Commission	www.explorestlouis.com

Washington DC Convention and Tourism Corporation | www.washington.org

PLATINUM SPONSORS

Hilton Hotels Corporation | www.hiltonworldwide.com
Hyatt Hotels Corporation | www.hyatt.com
MBNA America | www.mbna.com
Gaylord Hotels | www.gaylordhotels.com
Delta Air Lines | www.delta.com
Wachovia | www.wachovia.com

PLATINUM SPONSORS—CONVENTION AND VISITOR BUREAUS

Convention and Visitors Bureau of Greater Cleveland | www.travelcleveland.com
Dallas Convention & Visitors Bureau | www.dallascvb.com
Denver Metro Convention & Visitors Bureau, Inc. | www.denver.org
Hawaii Visitors & Convention Bureau | www.gohawaii.com
Indianapolis Convention and Visitors Association | www.indy.org
Irving Convention & Visitors Bureau | www.irvingtexas.com
Kansas City Convention & Visitors Association | www.visitkc.com
Greater Louisville Convention and Visitors Bureau | www.gotolouisville.com
Greater Milwaukee Convention & Visitors Bureau, Inc. | www.milwaukee.org
Greater Minneapolis Convention and Visitors Association | www.minneapolis.org
Orlando/Orange County Convention & Visitors Bureau, Inc. | www.orlandoinfo.com
Greater Phoenix Convention & Visitors Bureau | www.phoenixcvb.com
Puerto Rico Convention Bureau | www.meetpuertorico.com
San Francisco Convention & Visitors Bureau | www.sfvisitor.org

GOLD SPONSORS

American Airlines, Inc. | www.aa.com
Lang CPA Consulting (site under construction) | www.langcpa.com
The Langan Associates P.C., CPAs & Consultants | www.langancpa.com
Mohegan Sun | www.mohegansun.com
Unites Airlines | www.united.com
Results Direct | www.resultsdirect.com
The Signature Group, Inc. (TSG) | www.thesiggroup.com
SunTrust Bank | www.suntrust.com
Fairmont Hotels & Resorts | www.fairmont.com

| Wyndham International | www.wyndham.com |

SILVER SPONSORS

M&T Bank	www.mandtbank.com
AON Corporation	www.aon.com
Bostrom Corporation	www.bostrom.com
The Broadmoor	www.broadmoor.com
Cadmus	www.cadmus.com
CNA Insurance	www.cna.com
Colonial Williamsburg Company	www.history.org
Community Counseling Service Co., Inc.	www.fundraising.com
ExpoExchange	www.expoexchange.com
GES Exposition Services	www.ges.com
Hershey Resorts	www.hersheypa.com
Jenner and Block	www.jenner.com
Jones Lang LaSalle	www.joneslanglasalle.com
Loews Hotels	www.loewshotels.com
Marketing General, Inc.	www.marketinggeneral.com
The Masie Center	www.masie.com
The Olcott Consulting Group	www.olcottconsultinggroup.com
Outrigger Hotels and Resorts	www.outrigger.com
Peabody Hotel Group	www.peabodyhotelgroup.com
Plexus Consulting Group	www.plexusconsulting.com
The Ritz-Carlton Hotel Company, LLC	www.ritzcarlton.com
Ronald Reagan Building & International Trade Center Management Associates	www.itcdc.com
Tate and Tryon CPAs and Consultants	www.tatetryon.com
Tecker Consultants	www.tecker.com
Walt Disney Attractions, Inc.	www.disney.go.com

ASAE & The Center for Association Leadership's Strategic Research is transforming the future of associations. If you are interested in learning more, getting involved, or contributing, please e-mail strategicresearch@asaecenter.org.

Index

A

AARP, 32, 34, 43, 77

Ad Council of America, 60

Alliances, 60–62, 123–124

American College of Cardiology (ACC), 40–41, 47, 78

American Dental Association (ADA), 25, 41, 61–62, 79

Architecture, 45

ASAE & The Center for Association Leadership, vii, x–xi

Associated General Contractors (AGC), 26, 42, 50, 55–56, 80

Associations

    adaptability of, 55–59, 122–123

    alignment of products and services with mission, 13–14, 28–35, 119

    alliance building by, 60–62, 123–124

    attitude toward failure in, 33–35

    awareness of competition in, 43

    behaviors of, 74–75

    board of directors in, 64–65

    CEOs of, See CEOs

    commitments of, 12–14

    commitment to action, 53–62, 122–124

    commitment to analysis and feedback, 37–51, 120–122

    commitment to purpose, 23–35, 58–59, 118–119

    communication in, 44–48, 121

    competition versus cooperation in, 72

    concepts for greatness of, 19–21

    conventional wisdom in, 63–67

    core values of, 20–21

    culture of, 11–12, 20, 24–28, 69, 100–101, 106, 117, 118

structure of, 103–104
successful, *See* Remarkable associations
trade, 113–114
universities and, 61
vision of, 18–19
volunteers for, 57, 70

B

C

Culture, 11–12, 20, 24–28, 69, 100–101, 106, 117, 118
Customer-service culture
    American Dental Association, of, 25
    defined, 13, 24–25, 26, 117
    effects of, 26
    Girl Scouts of the USA (GSUSA), of, 26–27
    measuring, 11–12, 118
    Ohio Society of Certified Public Accountants (OSCPA), of, 28
    Society for Human Resource Management (SHRM), of, 41

D

Data analysis, 8–9, 40–44
Data-driven strategies, 38–44, 120–121
Data gathering, 6–8, 14, 42, 43, 95–110, 120
Democracy, 65
Dialogue, 44–48, 121
Discipline, xi, 20, 71–72

E

Economic slowdown, 55–56
Elections, 65
Engagement, 44–48

F

Failure, 33–35, 74
Farner, Elizabeth, xxii
Feuling, Bradley, xxii
Fifth Discipline Fieldbook, The, 71
Financial issues, 106–107
Financial reserves, 66–67
Focus groups, 118–119
For-profit companies, 66–67, 111

G

General Electric (GE), viii–ix
Girl Scout Research Institute, 39
Girl Scouts of the USA (GSUSA), 26–27, 29, 38–39, 48, 58, 60, 65, 81
Good to Great, xiv, 2, 19, 114

H

Hansen, Morten, ix–x
Historical matched-pair method, vii, viii–x, 68–72, 110